LEARN KOTLIN

Master Kotlin with Modern Architecture,
Coroutines, KMP,
Compose, and Professional Backend

Diego Rodrigues

LEARN KOTLIN
Master Kotlin with Modern Architecture, Coroutines, KMP, Compose, and Professional Backend

2025 Edition
Author: Diego Rodrigues
studiod21portoalegre@gmail.com

Published by StudioD21.

Important Note

The code and scripts presented in this book are primarily

intended to practically illustrate the concepts discussed throughout the chapters. They were developed to demonstrate didactic applications in controlled environments and may, therefore, require adjustments to function properly in different contexts. It is the reader's responsibility to validate the specific configurations of their development environment before practical implementation.

More than providing ready-made solutions, this book seeks to encourage a solid understanding of the fundamentals addressed, promoting critical thinking and technical autonomy. The examples presented should be seen as starting points for the reader to develop their own original solutions, adapted to the real demands of their career or projects. True technical competence arises from the ability to internalize essential principles and apply them creatively, strategically, and transformatively.

We encourage each reader to go beyond simply reproducing the examples, using this content as a foundation to build their own scripts and code, capable of generating significant impact in their professional journey. This is the spirit of applied knowledge: learning deeply to innovate with purpose.

Thank you for your trust, and we wish you a productive and inspiring study journey.

CONTENTS

GREETINGS!

Welcome to the 2025 edition of *Learn Kotlin* — a superior release, thoroughly revised, expanded, and optimized based on the TECHWRITE 2.3 Protocol. This book was designed to provide you with real technical mastery of the Kotlin language, combining didactic precision, practical clarity, and a carefully architected modular progression.

Throughout the chapters, you will embark on a learning journey guided by a professional curation of topics, fully explained code, reusable structures, and a strong focus on direct application. This edition significantly surpasses the previous one by expanding its scope, deepening strategic topics, and incorporating the latest practices in multiplatform, backend, and mobile development.

With technical rigor and refined writing, this book was made not just for you to learn Kotlin, but to master its application with confidence, elegance, and purpose.

ABOUT THE AUTHOR

Diego Rodrigues
Technical Author and Independent Researcher
ORCID: https://orcid.org/0009-0006-2178-634X
StudioD21 Smart Tech Content & Intell Systems
Email: studiod21portoalegre@gmail.com
LinkedIn: www.linkedin.com/in/diegoxpertai

An international technical author (tech writer) focused on structured production of applied knowledge. Founder of StudioD21 Smart Tech Content & Intell Systems, where he leads the creation of intelligent frameworks and the publication of didactic technical books supported by artificial intelligence, such as the *Kali Linux Extreme* series, *SMARTBOOKS D21*, among others.

Holder of 42 international certifications issued by institutions such as IBM, Google, Microsoft, AWS, Cisco, META, Ec-Council, Palo Alto, and Boston University, he operates in the fields of Artificial Intelligence, Machine Learning, Data Science, Big Data, Blockchain, Connectivity Technologies, Ethical Hacking, and Threat Intelligence.

Since 2003, he has developed over 200 technical projects for brands in Brazil, the USA, and Mexico. In 2024, he established himself as one of the leading technical authors of the new generation, with more than 180 titles published in six languages. His work is based on his proprietary applied technical writing protocol TECHWRITE 2.2, aimed at scalability, conceptual precision, and practical applicability in professional environments.

BOOK PRESENTATION

The technical journey proposed in this manual begins with the conceptual foundations of the Kotlin language, covering its history, interoperability with Java, and its application ecosystems. Next, you will be guided through the setup of the development environment with IntelliJ IDEA and Android Studio, focusing on productivity, project organization, and configuration best practices.

Advancing in the language structure, the book presents Kotlin's fundamental constructs: variable declaration, type inference, functions, primitive types, and flow control using idiomatic structures such as if, when, for, and while. The construction and use of functions are highlighted with default parameters, lambdas, inline functions, and the use of scopes like let, run, and apply, promoting clarity and functional encapsulation.

Next, you dive into collection handling, using lists, sets, maps, and their respective functional operations with map, filter, groupBy, along with the use of sequences for efficiency and immutability. Modeling with classes and objects, constructors, properties, methods, and instantiation forms the basis of object-oriented programming, which is extended with inheritance, overriding, applied polymorphism, and the conscious use of the open modifier.

Interfaces, abstract classes, and multiplatform contracts are explored with attention to reuse patterns, responsibility separation, and safe composition. String manipulation receives special focus, including interpolation, multiline strings, regular expressions, and native transformation methods.

File operations, reading and writing with buffers, binary streams, and efficient handling of large data volumes form the core of disk persistence. In error control flow, you will master try, catch, finally blocks, custom exceptions, and robust validation strategies.

The conceptual review of object orientation is expanded with a focus on encapsulation, modularity, and architectural patterns, soon evolving into an introduction to functional programming with functions as first-class citizens, composition, immutability, and operators such as reduce and fold.

From there, the book delves into asynchronous programming with coroutines, covering launch, async, await, withContext, and the efficient use of Dispatchers to build non-blocking code. Integration with REST APIs becomes fluid with Retrofit and Ktor, asynchronous request handling, JWT authentication, and advanced JSON processing.

Local storage is handled using SQLite and Room, with CRUD operations, relationship modeling, and optimized query execution. To ensure reliability, the book introduces automated testing with a focus on JUnit 5, MockK, integration tests, and code validation strategies.

The technical scope expands into multiplatform development with Kotlin Multiplatform (KMP), where you share code across Android, iOS, and backend using the strategic use of expect and actual. In parallel, Android app development is explored in depth: lifecycle, ViewBinding, usage of RecyclerView, and creation of fluid animations based on UI events.

On the backend, you build modern APIs with Ktor, defining routes, middlewares, JWT authentication, error handling, and database integration via DSL. Project organization and management are strengthened with Gradle Kotlin DSL, modularization, centralized versioning, and build optimization.

Toward the final stretch, the book presents code standards,

refactoring, style, naming conventions, applied design patterns, and layered architecture. It then guides the publication of libraries to Maven Central, signing with GPG, automatic documentation with Dokka, and professional distribution strategies.

The work concludes by leading the reader through a strategic overview of Kotlin's future: multiplatform adoption, the rise of Jetpack Compose, integration with WebAssembly, and growing use in artificial intelligence, blockchain, IoT, and distributed systems. This vision enables today's technical decisions to align with tomorrow's technological demands.

This book is more than a technical guide — it is a practical and strategic foundation for anyone who seeks fluency in Kotlin, with real mastery over its application in the modern world of software engineering.

CHAPTER 1. INTRODUCTION TO KOTLIN

Kotlin is a modern, stable language that is increasingly adopted for the development of robust and scalable applications. It was created to solve real-world problems faced by developers in Android development, backends, cross-platform systems, and modern applications that demand productivity without compromising performance.

Its main differentiator lies in the balance between conciseness and safety. Kotlin significantly reduces the verbosity of traditional languages like Java while reinforcing control over common errors, such as the infamous NullPointerException. This means less code, fewer bugs, and greater readability — three elements that directly impact the productivity of any project.

Companies of all sizes adopt Kotlin in production solutions. It is fully interoperable with Java, allowing legacy systems to be migrated gradually. In addition, it can be used for mobile applications (especially Android), backend development with frameworks such as Ktor, as well as web applications via Kotlin/JS and cross-platform apps via Kotlin Multiplatform.

Basic Execution with Code

The language relies on a simple and expressive syntax. A minimal program in Kotlin requires few lines to be functional. Below is the equivalent to the classic "Hello, World!":

kotlin

```
fun main() {
    println("Hello, Kotlin!")
}
```

The main function is the entry point of any Kotlin application. The println function sends the message to the console. There's no need to define a class just to start a program, as is required in Java. This reduces overhead for beginners and accelerates development.

The same conciseness applies to variable declarations:

kotlin

```
val name = "John"
var age = 30
```

Using val indicates an immutable variable, while var allows for modification. Kotlin automatically infers the variable type, increasing fluency in writing without sacrificing strong typing.

Functional Variations

Kotlin offers multiple ways to express logic, always with a focus on clarity. Function creation, for example, can be done traditionally or in a single-expression format:

Standard form:

kotlin

```
fun sum(a: Int, b: Int): Int {
    return a + b
}
```

Reduced form:

kotlin

```kotlin
fun sum(a: Int, b: Int) = a + b
```

Both produce the same result. The choice depends on the complexity of the function and the team's preferred style. This level of freedom allows the code to adapt to the project context without compromising technical standards.

Kotlin also integrates safely with null type systems. A direct example:

kotlin

```kotlin
fun textLength(text: String?): Int {
    return text?.length ?: 0
}
```

This code returns the length of a string if it is not null. Otherwise, it returns zero. The language forces the programmer to deal with nullability at the declaration moment, which drastically reduces runtime failures.

System Behavior

During execution of a Kotlin program, system behavior may vary depending on the use of null typing, collections, coroutines, and Java library interactions.

Using println sends information directly to the standard console. Functions involving file reading, networking, or database access require the use of coroutines or exception handling.

When Kotlin code is compiled for the JVM, it generates bytecode compatible with Java. This means any Kotlin code can run on Java virtual machines, and Java libraries can be used without any adaptation.

If an attempt is made to access a null property without proper verification, Kotlin halts execution with a clear exception, facilitating diagnosis. For example:

kotlin

```
val name: String? = null

println(name!!.length) // Exception:
KotlinNullPointerException
```

The !! operator forces dereferencing a null value. Its use should be avoided outside controlled contexts.

Control and Monitoring

To track Kotlin executions in real-time, one can use print, println, logging via libraries like SLF4J, or on Android applications, Logcat. Monitoring null values, lifecycles, and coroutine outputs should be done with real-time debugging inspections.

Another important tool is kotlin-reflect, which allows for class introspection, useful for frameworks and dynamic validations. On the backend, logs can be configured directly on servers or stored in tools like ELK Stack.

Kotlin can also be monitored via automated tests using JUnit and MockK, ensuring the application behaves as expected continuously.

Common Error Resolution

- Trying to access null properties without proper handling

Solution: Use ?., ?:, or explicit checks

- Using var where val would be safer
  Solution: Prefer val for immutability and safety

- Confusing type inference with dynamic typing
  Solution: Kotlin is statically typed; use is and as consciously

- Importing Java classes incompatible with expected nullability
  Solution: Add explicit checks when integrating legacy code

- Forgetting that default collections are immutable
  Solution: Use mutableListOf, mutableMapOf when needed

Best Practices

- Prefer val over var whenever possible

- Use pure functions and simple expressions

- Avoid !! — use native null safety

- Organize code into small, cohesive functions

- Use data class to represent models with value-based equality

- Adopt when instead of multiple if-else blocks

- Name variables clearly and avoid excessive abbreviations

- Use scope functions like apply, let, and run in moderation

- Document complex functions with KDoc

- Use automated tests to validate expected behavior

Strategic Summary

Kotlin was designed based on developers' practical experience. It solves real-world problems directly without compromising robustness. The language combines readability, safety, and interoperability, making it a solid choice for both beginners and seasoned professionals.

Its learning curve is short, but its potential is deep. From simple scripts to complete platforms with multiple modules, Kotlin delivers performance and elegance. By mastering its syntax, understanding null control mechanisms, applying scope functions, and following best practices, developers build cleaner, scalable, and more reliable solutions.

From this point on, the journey becomes technical and practical. The language has been introduced. Now, the focus will be on applying it to real scenarios, step by step, until professional mastery is achieved.

CHAPTER 2. SETTING UP THE DEVELOPMENT ENVIRONMENT

To develop with Kotlin productively and fluently, the development environment must be properly structured from the beginning. The language offers native support for multiple platforms — Android, backend, desktop, web, and multiplatform — but this versatility only translates into efficiency when the project foundation is built with the right tools, properly configured, and with dependencies managed in a stable way.

The first step is choosing the IDE. IntelliJ IDEA, from JetBrains, is the main choice for those working with Kotlin, offering native support, intelligent suggestions, integration with build tools, and advanced refactoring features. For mobile development, especially Android, Android Studio is the best option — derived from IntelliJ, it comes with the necessary Kotlin plugins and full integration with the Android SDK.

In IntelliJ IDEA, when starting a new project, select the "Kotlin" option and choose the project type, such as "Kotlin/JVM." Then, define the project name, destination directory, and configure the SDK. If there is no JDK installed, the IDE itself offers the option to download and configure it automatically. The generated structure includes the main function already ready for execution:

kotlin

```
fun main() {
```

```
    println("Environment successfully configured!")
}
```

This code can be run directly from the IDE and serves as an initial validation of the Kotlin environment.

In Android Studio, creating a new project follows a visual wizard. Choose a template like "Empty Activity," select Kotlin as the default language, define the minimum API version and the package name. The created structure includes a MainActivity.kt, XML layout files, and Gradle as the build system. The basic code is already functional and ready to run in the emulator.

Both IDEs offer code suggestions, shortcuts, automated refactorings, and integration with version control systems like Git. The built-in terminal and plugin support allow transforming the environment into a productivity hub.

Useful plugins include:

- **Kotlin Plugin**: already installed by default, responsible for interpreting and compiling .kt files
- **Key Promoter X**: displays shortcut tips when using the mouse

- **GitToolBox**: enhances Git integration with real-time status

- **Rainbow Brackets**: makes reading nested code blocks easier

For multiplatform projects, it's possible to select the "Kotlin Multiplatform" template and define the desired targets, such as JVM, Android, JS, or iOS. The project structure will be segmented into commonMain, androidMain, iosMain, and other code blocks specific to each platform, allowing for reuse of central logic.

Dependency and configuration management is done with Gradle, preferably using the Kotlin DSL format (build.gradle.kts). A minimal project requires at least the standard language dependency:

kotlin

```
dependencies {
    implementation(kotlin("stdlib"))
}
```

The IDE automatically synchronizes these configurations and allows the application to be compiled with one click.

To validate the environment outside the IDE as well, the Kotlin compiler can be installed separately. After that, .kt files can be compiled with:

bash

```
kotlinc MeuArquivo.kt -include-runtime -d MeuArquivo.jar
```

And run with:

bash

```
java -jar MeuArquivo.jar
```

This approach is especially useful for scripts, automation, and integration with CI/CD pipelines.

In Android projects, it is important to properly configure the emulators. Android Studio allows you to create virtual devices with different screen sizes, resolutions, and Android versions. Running the application on these emulators is done directly via the IDE's "Run" button, validating the application flow from compilation to interaction with the virtual operating system.

In addition to graphical tools, properly configuring Version Control in the IDE speeds up team workflows. Native Git integration allows commits, merges, change history, and branch creation directly from the side panel.

Complementary static analysis tools should be added at the beginning of the project. Detekt and Ktlint are the most used:

kotlin

```
plugins {
    id("io.gitlab.arturbosch.detekt") version "1.23.0"
}
```

With them, code is automatically inspected at each build, pointing out possible standard violations and facilitating the maintenance of the technical base.

Common Error Resolution

- Kotlin does not appear as an option when creating a new project
  Solution: Enable the Kotlin plugin in the IDE settings

- Compilation error due to missing JDK configuration
  Solution: Install a compatible JDK and define the path at File > Project Structure > SDKs

- Android app fails to run in emulator
  Solution: Check if the virtual device is properly initialized and if the minimum API is compatible

- Declared dependency not recognized

Solution: Confirm that the project was synchronized after modifying build.gradle.kts

- Kotlin not recognized in the terminal
  Solution: Check if the compiler is installed and if the executable path is added to the system's PATH

Best Practices

- Use IntelliJ IDEA for multiplatform projects and Android Studio for mobile applications

- Prefer the build.gradle.kts format for type-safe configuration and language integration

- Configure Version Control as soon as the project starts and commit frequently

- Use keyboard shortcuts whenever possible to speed up navigation and execution

- Install useful plugins like Key Promoter X and Detekt for productivity and analysis

- Validate the Kotlin configuration by compiling and running a simple program before adding external dependencies

- Document the project structure and the purpose of each module from the beginning

- Keep the Kotlin Plugin updated in the IDE to avoid compatibility issues

- Enable the IDE's automatic lint to avoid formatting and code standard issues

- Add an .editorconfig file to the project to standardize rules among different developers

Strategic Summary

Setting up the Kotlin development environment goes far beyond simply installing the IDE. It defines the rhythm, stability, and scalability of the project from the very first steps. A well-structured environment eliminates trivial errors, accelerates development, and directly supports the application of professional best practices. Mastering the structure, IDE usage, dependency management, and execution validation is a mandatory technical prerequisite for any Kotlin developer aiming for professional performance.

CHAPTER 3. BASIC SYNTAX AND PROGRAM STRUCTURE

Kotlin's syntax is designed to be clear, concise, and safe. Its structure favors readability and reduces the need for repetitive code. From the first declarations to the definition of reusable functions, each language construct offers a combination of expressiveness and control that facilitates development and simplifies code maintenance.

The language uses type inference to reduce verbosity without giving up the static type system. This means that the compiler deduces the type of the variable from the assigned value, while the program remains safe and validated at compile time.

The minimum structure of a functional Kotlin program consists of a main function and variable declarations:

kotlin

```kotlin
fun main() {
    val language = "Kotlin"
    println("Learning $language efficiently")
}
```

The fun main() block defines the entry point of the application. The println command sends the message to the console. The variable language is declared with val, indicating that its value will not change. Kotlin automatically recognizes the String type, making the explicit annotation unnecessary.

Variables in Kotlin are divided into two main groups: immutable, declared with val, and mutable, declared with var. Using val is preferred whenever the variable does not need to be modified, which reinforces code safety and predictability.

kotlin

```kotlin
val name = "John"
var age = 28
```

In the declaration above, name will always be "John", while age can be reassigned during execution:

kotlin

```kotlin
age = 29
```

Variable types can be inferred or explicitly declared:

kotlin

```kotlin
val weight: Double = 74.5
val height = 1.82
```

Both declarations behave the same. Inference favors writing speed, while explicit declaration is useful for documentation and readability.

Available primitive types include:

- Int for integers

- Double and Float for decimal numbers

- Boolean for true or false

- Char for single characters

- String for text

Function structure is defined by the keyword fun, followed by the function name, parameters, and return type:

kotlin

```kotlin
fun greeting(name: String): String {
    return "Hello, $name!"
}
```

The function above receives a String as a parameter and returns another String with a personalized greeting. Kotlin allows simplification for single-expression return functions:

kotlin

```kotlin
fun greeting(name: String) = "Hello, $name!"
```

This format is valid when the function body consists of a single expression.

Functions without a return use the Unit type, which can be omitted:

kotlin

```kotlin
fun showMessage(message: String) {
    println(message)
}
```

Flow control is done with structures like if, when, for, while, and do-while. The if construct works both as an expression and a conditional block:

kotlin

```kotlin
val status = if (age >= 18) "Adult" else "Minor"
```

The when construct replaces switch blocks with more flexibility:

kotlin

```kotlin
fun evaluateGrade(grade: Int): String {
    return when (grade) {
        in 9..10 -> "Excellent"
        in 7..8 -> "Good"
        in 5..6 -> "Fair"
        else -> "Poor"
    }
}
```

Loop structures are used to iterate over collections, ranges, or conditions:

kotlin

```kotlin
for (i in 1..5) {
    println("Counting: $i")
}
```

The while loop continues running as long as the condition is true:

kotlin

```kotlin
var counter = 0
while (counter < 3) {
    println("Value: $counter")
    counter++
}
```

The do-while loop ensures the block executes at least once:

kotlin

```kotlin
var attempt = 1
do {
    println("Attempt $attempt")
    attempt++
} while (attempt <= 3)
```

Kotlin also supports descending ranges with downTo and steps with step:

kotlin

```kotlin
for (i in 10 downTo 1 step 2) {
    println(i)
}
```

String interpolation is one of the most efficient tools for composing dynamic messages:

kotlin

```kotlin
val product = "Laptop"
```

```
val price = 3250.90
println("The product $product costs R$ $price")
```

Functions can have optional parameters with default values:

kotlin

```
fun showMessage(text: String = "Default message") {
    println(text)
}
```

Calling showMessage() without arguments will display the default text.

Kotlin also allows functions to be declared inside other functions, known as local functions. This is useful when the inner logic won't be used outside that scope:

kotlin

```
fun calculateTotal(items: List<Double>): Double {
    fun applyDiscount(value: Double): Double = value * 0.9
    return items.sum().let { applyDiscount(it) }
}
```

Scope functions such as let, apply, run, also, and with help organize code more expressively, especially when working with objects:

kotlin

```
val user = User().apply {
    name = "Anna"
```

```
    age = 34
}
```

This construct allows an object to be configured at creation time, reducing the number of chained calls.

Kotlin also supports immutable and mutable collections, which will be explored further later. For now, basic syntax allows lists to be created directly:

kotlin

```
val colors = listOf("blue", "green", "red")
```

And mutable lists:

kotlin

```
val numbers = mutableListOf(1, 2, 3)
numbers.add(4)
```

The main mathematical and logical operations follow the same structure as in other languages:

kotlin

```
val sum = 10 + 5
val valid = sum > 10 && sum < 20
```

The language's clarity allows complex logic blocks to be composed intuitively while maintaining readability even in denser structures.

Common Error Resolution

- Using var where val would ensure immutability
  Solution: Prefer val whenever there's no need to change the value

- Omitting explicit type in ambiguous contexts
  Solution: Declare the type when inference is not clear

- Forgetting return in functions with declared return type
  Solution: Ensure functions with : Type have a return or are in expression format

- Using long if chains instead of when
  Solution: Refactor to when when there are multiple conditions based on the same value

- Accessing null variables without null-checking
  Solution: Use ?. and ?: operators to handle potentially null values

Best Practices

- Prefer val over var to ensure code stability

- Give descriptive names to variables and functions, avoiding generic abbreviations

- Use small functions with a single, well-defined responsibility

- Centralize constants and fixed values in config objects or separate files

- Use string interpolation when composing dynamic messages

- Declare functions in reduced form when logic is simple

- Avoid duplicate code using reusable functions

- Use when when there are multiple conditional comparisons

- Document functions clearly, especially public ones

- Organize functions in separate files by responsibility domain

Strategic Summary

Kotlin's basic syntax offers all the essential features to write clean, safe, and efficient programs. By combining static typing with smart inference, expressive control structures, reusable functions, and scope best practices, the language enables agile and professional development. Mastering this technical foundation is essential for safely advancing into the construction of more complex and robust solutions.

CHAPTER 4. FLOW CONTROL

Flow control in Kotlin is an essential tool for creating programs that react to conditions, repeat tasks, and make decisions dynamically. The language offers modern idiomatic structures that replace traditional instructions with more readable and safer constructs. Available tools include the if, when conditionals and the for, while, and do-while loops — all compatible with expressions that return values.

The if structure evaluates a boolean condition and executes different blocks depending on the result. In Kotlin, if can be used as an expression, returning values directly:

kotlin

```kotlin
val status = if (age >= 18) "Adult" else "Minor"
```

This eliminates the need for auxiliary variables and makes the code more concise. For multiple conditions, chained else if statements enable complex decisions with syntactic clarity:

kotlin

```kotlin
val classification = if (grade >= 90) "Excellent"
    else if (grade >= 70) "Good"
    else if (grade >= 50) "Fair"
    else "Insufficient"
```

The when replaces long blocks of if-else with elegance. It

evaluates a variable or expression, offering multiple execution paths:

kotlin

```kotlin
fun evaluateGrade(grade: Int): String {
    return when (grade) {
        in 90..100 -> "Excellent"
        in 70..89 -> "Good"
        in 50..69 -> "Fair"
        else -> "Insufficient"
    }
}
```

Besides fixed values and ranges, when can handle types:

kotlin

```kotlin
fun identifyType(value: Any): String {
    return when (value) {
        is Int -> "Integer"
        is String -> "Text"
        is Boolean -> "Boolean"
        else -> "Unknown"
    }
}
```

In repetition control, for iterates over ranges, collections, and sequences. Its syntax favors direct readability:

kotlin

```kotlin
for (i in 1..5) {
    println("Counting: $i")
}
```

With step, the iteration step can be defined:

kotlin
```kotlin
for (i in 0..10 step 2) {
    println(i)
}
```

For reverse loops, downTo allows descending iteration:

kotlin
```kotlin
for (i in 5 downTo 1) {
    println(i)
}
```

The while loop executes repeatedly while the condition is true:

kotlin
```kotlin
var counter = 0
while (counter < 3) {
    println("Value: $counter")
    counter++
}
```

The do-while loop ensures the block is executed at least once:

kotlin

```kotlin
var attempt = 1
do {
    println("Attempt: $attempt")
    attempt++
} while (attempt <= 3)
```

Kotlin's great advantage lies in allowing control structures to be expressions with return values, promoting a more functional approach:

kotlin

```kotlin
val parity = if (number % 2 == 0) "Even" else "Odd"
```

This also applies to when:

kotlin

```kotlin
val result = when {
    age < 12 -> "Child"
    age in 12..17 -> "Teenager"
    age >= 18 -> "Adult"
    else -> "Invalid age"
}
```

These constructs make the code more straightforward and reduce the creation of intermediate variables.

Common Error Resolution

- Using cascading if when when would be clearer
  Solution: Replace with when using multiple direct clauses

- Forgetting to use step when creating custom intervals
  Solution: Add step explicitly to avoid infinite loops or
  incorrect logic

- Confusing while with do-while, expecting execution
  without the condition being met
  Solution: Verify if execution must happen at least once,
  then use do-while

- Evaluating ranges with == instead of in
  Solution: Use in to check if a value is within a range (value
  in 1..10)

- Handling types in when without ensuring type safety
  afterward
  Solution: Use safe casts or ensure closed scope for the type
  within the when block

Best Practices

- Use val for results of if and when expressions

- Use when with multiple values per line to avoid repetition

- Avoid infinite loops without clearly defined exit
  conditions

- Prefer downTo and step when managing loops with
  custom increments

- Declare variables within the scope of the for loop to avoid state leakage

- Avoid complex logic inside conditions; extract it to helper functions

- Document when expressions with multiple rules to aid maintenance

- Use string interpolation in println blocks for readability

- Validate range limits before using them in for loops

- Leverage direct returns in if and when to eliminate redundant return statements

Strategic Summary

Mastering flow control structures in Kotlin is fundamental for developing efficient, clear, and expressive algorithms. With features like returning if expressions, multifunctional when, loops with precise control, and idiomatic syntax, the language provides everything necessary to control program execution in a modern way. By focusing on clarity and expression-based constructs, it's possible to write more concise, direct, and professional code, maximizing productivity and reducing logical errors.

CHAPTER 5. FUNCTIONS AND SCOPES

Functions are fundamental units of reuse, organization, and readability in Kotlin. The language embraces a functional and expressive approach, allowing the creation of lean, parameterizable functions with controlled scopes. From basic functions with default parameters to lambdas, inline functions, and scope blocks like let, apply, run, also, and with, Kotlin's structure favors clarity and encapsulation.

Function creation starts with the keyword fun, followed by the name, parameters, and return type:

kotlin

```kotlin
fun greeting(name: String): String {
    return "Hello, $name!"
}
```

Kotlin allows this declaration to be further reduced when the function has only one expression:

kotlin

```kotlin
fun greeting(name: String) = "Hello, $name!"
```

This format is concise and widely used for utility functions, where simplicity enhances readability.

Default parameters are declared directly in the function signature, avoiding unnecessary overloads:

kotlin

```kotlin
fun showMessage(text: String = "Default message") {
    println(text)
}
```

Calling showMessage() without arguments will display "Default message". When the argument is provided, it replaces the default value. This makes the code leaner and reduces duplication.

Kotlin supports functions with a variable number of arguments using the vararg modifier. This allows receiving multiple values of the same type:

kotlin

```kotlin
fun sum(vararg numbers: Int): Int {
    return numbers.sum()
}
```

The function above can be called with any number of integer arguments, which will automatically be converted into an internal array.

Lambdas are function expressions that can be stored in variables, passed as arguments, and returned from other functions. The basic syntax is:

kotlin

```kotlin
val double = { x: Int -> x * 2 }

println(double(4)) // 8
```

Lambdas can also be used in higher-order functions like map, filter, forEach:

kotlin

```kotlin
val numbers = listOf(1, 2, 3, 4)
val evens = numbers.filter { it % 2 == 0 }
```

In this context, it represents the current item in the list. The use of lambdas with utility functions is one of Kotlin's most powerful features.

Inline functions are declared with the inline modifier to optimize performance in lambda calls. When a function is marked as inline, the compiler substitutes the call with the actual implementation at the usage point:

kotlin

```kotlin
inline fun execute(action: () -> Unit) {
    println("Start")
    action()
    println("End")
}
```

This practice reduces call overhead, especially in higher-order functions, and is common in Kotlin libraries for performance-critical code.

Scope functions allow operations to be applied on objects within a defined block, returning useful results without leaving the context. The main ones are:

let: executes a block with the object as it, returns the last expression's result

kotlin

```kotlin
val name: String? = "Carlos"
name?.let {
    println("Name with value: $it")
}
```

apply: returns the object after applying operations using this

kotlin

```kotlin
val config = Configuration().apply {
    port = 8080
    protocol = "HTTP"
}
```

run: similar to let, but uses this as context and returns the last line

kotlin

```kotlin
val result = "Data".run {
    uppercase()
}
```

also: like let, but returns the original object; useful for debugging or logging

kotlin

```kotlin
val user = User().also {
    println("Object created: $it")
```

```
}
```

with: common when the object cannot be null and multiple operations need to be applied without returning a transformation

kotlin

```kotlin
val sb = StringBuilder()
with(sb) {
    append("Line 1\n")
    append("Line 2\n")
}
```

These functions help keep code organized, avoiding variable name repetition and maintaining visually limited scopes.

It is also possible to declare functions inside other functions. These are called local functions and are useful for organizing complex internal logic:

kotlin

```kotlin
fun calculate(value: Int): Int {
    fun double(x: Int) = x * 2
    return double(value)
}
```

Besides controlled visibility, this feature reduces pollution of the application's global scope.

Functions can be assigned to variables, passed as arguments, and even returned from other functions:

kotlin

```kotlin
fun operation(): (Int) -> Int {
    return { it * it }
}
val result = operation()(5) // 25
```

This usage makes functions first-class citizens, allowing highly modular and expressive programming styles.

Common Error Resolution

- Declaring a function without a return type and without return
  Solution: Declare Unit or add a compatible return value

- Using apply where a transformed return is needed
  Solution: Replace with run or let when return matters

- Defining a lambda but not using it properly within the function scope
  Solution: Ensure the lambda is called within the function

- Trying to use external variables in inline lambdas without control
  Solution: Ensure the lambda is crossinline if it cannot be returned

- Confusing this and it scopes when nesting scope functions
  Solution: Separate blocks or explicitly name parameters to avoid ambiguity

Best Practices

- Use single-expression functions for simple logic

- Declare default parameters to avoid excessive overloads

- Use apply to configure objects, let for transformations, and also for tracking

- Keep lambdas short and direct; extract larger logic into named functions

- Organize related functions into separate files or objects

- Name functions with action verbs that clearly express their purpose

- Specify return types when the function is part of a public API

- Minimize side effects within scope functions

- Use inline only when performance gain is proven

- Avoid excessive nesting of functions to maintain readability

Strategic Summary

Functions are the core of any Kotlin application. With support for concise expressions, default parameters, lambdas, controlled scopes, and inline optimizations, the language provides one of the most sophisticated environments for functional and object-oriented programming. By mastering the construction and use of these functions, developers gain control, expressiveness, and flexibility to build efficient, readable, and highly reusable applications.

CHAPTER 6. WORKING WITH COLLECTIONS

Kotlin offers an extremely powerful collections API, designed to manipulate data in a fluid, safe, and expressive manner. The language supports lists, sets, and maps, and allows for transformations using functional operations such as map, filter, groupBy, and reduce. Additionally, the use of sequences optimizes processing of large data volumes by applying lazy transformations.

Collections in Kotlin are divided into two major groups: immutable and mutable. Immutable ones are created with functions like listOf, setOf, and mapOf, while mutable collections are created with mutableListOf, mutableSetOf, and mutableMapOf.

Creating lists is straightforward:

kotlin

```
val names = listOf("Ana", "Carlos", "Beatriz")
```

This list is immutable, meaning it cannot be modified. To modify elements, use:

kotlin

```
val tasks = mutableListOf("Write", "Test", "Refactor")
tasks.add("Publish")
```

Indices start at zero and elements can be accessed with tasks[0]. Sets store only unique values, ignoring duplicates:

kotlin

```
val categories = setOf("Book", "Video", "Article", "Book")
println(categories.size) // 3
```

For mutable sets:

kotlin

```
val roles = mutableSetOf("admin", "editor")
roles.add("reader")
```

Maps associate keys with values:

kotlin

```
val users = mapOf(1 to "John", 2 to "Maria")
println(users[2]) // Maria
```

To edit:

kotlin

```
val settings = mutableMapOf("mode" to "dark")
settings["volume"] = "high"
```

Collection manipulation is elevated by transformation functions. map transforms elements, creating a new collection based on a function:

kotlin

```kotlin
val numbers = listOf(1, 2, 3)
val doubled = numbers.map { it * 2 }
```

filter selects elements based on a condition:

kotlin

```kotlin
val evens = numbers.filter { it % 2 == 0 }
```

groupBy organizes elements into groups based on a key:

kotlin

```kotlin
val products = listOf("Coffee", "Tea", "Meat", "Rice")
val grouped = products.groupBy { it.first() }
```

The result is a map where keys are initial letters and values are lists of words starting with that letter.

Functions like any, all, none, count, firstOrNull, lastOrNull, and find allow expressive collection queries:

kotlin

```kotlin
val hasEvens = numbers.any { it % 2 == 0 }
val allOdd = numbers.all { it % 2 != 0 }
val noneNegative = numbers.none { it < 0 }
val countGreaterThanOne = numbers.count { it > 1 }
```

For large collections, the use of sequence is recommended. Sequences perform transformations lazily, avoiding creation of intermediate collections:

kotlin

```kotlin
val result = numbers.asSequence()
    .filter { it > 1 }
    .map { it * 10 }
    .toList()
```

This pipeline executes only when needed, reducing memory consumption and improving performance.

Functions like fold and reduce allow value aggregation:

kotlin

```kotlin
val sum = numbers.fold(0) { acc, number -> acc + number }
val product = numbers.reduce { acc, number -> acc * number }
```

While fold allows initializing an accumulator value, reduce uses the first element of the collection as the starting point.

Collection sorting can be done with sorted, sortedBy, reversed, shuffled:

kotlin

```kotlin
val sorted = numbers.sortedDescending()
```

distinct removes duplicate elements:

kotlin

```kotlin
val data = listOf(1, 2, 2, 3, 3, 3)
val uniques = data.distinct()
```

Combining map with flatten transforms nested lists into a

single one:

kotlin

```
val lists = listOf(listOf(1, 2), listOf(3, 4))
val combined = lists.flatten()
```

For safety, Kotlin provides extensions like getOrElse and getOrNull:

kotlin

```
val item = names.getOrNull(5) ?: "Invalid"
```

These strategies prevent exceptions caused by accessing nonexistent indices.

Common Error Resolution

- Trying to modify immutable lists with .add()
  Solution: Use mutableListOf when data needs to be modified

- Using map without calling toList() afterward
  Solution: End pipelines with toList() when using sequence or chained operations

- Accessing a nonexistent index directly with brackets
  Solution: Use getOrNull() with a default value or check the list size

- Confusing groupBy with associateBy
  Solution: groupBy creates a map with value lists; associateBy maps keys to a single value

- Forgetting to convert from sequence to concrete collection Solution: End the pipeline with toList() or toSet() to get a usable result

Best Practices

- Use immutable collections whenever data doesn't need to be changed

- Prefer functional operations (map, filter, fold) for readability and efficiency

- Apply sequence when working with large collections or chained pipelines

- Name variables descriptively, even in simple lambdas (e.g., value, element)

- Avoid excessive use of .forEach — prioritize pure functions

- Use groupBy to organize data before applying mass operations

- Handle accesses with getOrNull or null-coalescing operators

- Chain operations clearly, keeping each step well-defined

- Create helper functions when chained operations become too complex

- Always validate if the data volume justifies using sequence to avoid unnecessary overhead

Strategic Summary

Working with collections in Kotlin is a key technical advantage. The language's API promotes elegant, concise, and safe transformations. From simple lists to complex data pipelines with sequence, mastering these structures enables writing cleaner, more predictable, and efficient code. The combination of immutable collections with functional operations provides a powerful foundation for building modern applications, where clarity, performance, and maintainability go hand in hand.

CHAPTER 7. CLASSES AND OBJECTS

Kotlin is an object-oriented language that offers a modern and concise syntax for declaring classes, properties, constructors, and methods. Creating and manipulating objects in Kotlin is designed to be practical, safe, and highly expressive. From simple structures to more complex architectures, the language's class model encourages encapsulation, reusability, and clarity.

A basic class declaration can be done in a single line:

kotlin

```
class User
```

This structure creates a class with no properties or behavior. To make it useful, properties and constructors are added. Kotlin allows defining the primary constructor directly in the class signature:

kotlin

```
class User(val name: String, var age: Int)
```

This form automatically creates two properties (name and age) and a constructor. To instantiate an object of this class, simply pass the expected values:

kotlin

```kotlin
val user = User("Carlos", 30)
println(user.name) // Carlos
```

The val modifier creates immutable (read-only) properties, while var allows later modification:

kotlin

```kotlin
user.age = 31
```

Properties can also be declared internally with initialization logic:

kotlin

```kotlin
class Product(name: String, price: Double) {
    val formattedName = name.uppercase()
    var priceWithTax = price * 1.15
}
```

In this case, the properties are calculated at object creation time, with custom logic.

Kotlin supports secondary constructors for situations where multiple creation methods are needed:

kotlin

```kotlin
class Client {
    var name: String
    var age: Int

    constructor(name: String) {
```

```kotlin
        this.name = name
        this.age = 0
    }


    constructor(name: String, age: Int) {
        this.name = name
        this.age = age
    }
}
```

The recommendation, however, is to prioritize the use of the primary constructor with default values:

kotlin

```kotlin
class Client(val name: String, val age: Int = 0)
```

Methods are functions declared inside a class. They define the object's behavior:

kotlin

```kotlin
class Circle(val radius: Double) {
    fun area(): Double = Math.PI * radius * radius
}
```

To access or execute these methods:

kotlin

```kotlin
val c = Circle(2.0)
```

```
println(c.area()) // 12.566...
```

Kotlin uses the init keyword for initialization blocks. This block is executed automatically after the constructor:

kotlin

```
class Session(val user: String) {
    init {
        println("Session started for $user")
    }
}
```

Modifiers like open, final, abstract, and sealed control inheritance and class behavior:

- **open**: allows the class to be inherited

- **final**: blocks inheritance (default)

- **abstract**: requires the class to be inherited and methods to be implemented

- **sealed**: limits inheritance to a controlled set of subclasses

Properties can have their own custom getters and setters:

kotlin

```
class Item {
    var quantity: Int = 0
        set(value) {
            field = if (value < 0) 0 else value
```

```
   }
}
```

The keyword field refers to the internal value of the property.

Objects are instances of classes. Kotlin simplifies the creation of unique objects with object, which automatically defines singletons:

kotlin

```
object Configuration {
   val version = "1.0"
}
```

This object can be accessed without instantiation:

kotlin

```
println(Configuration.version)
```

Anonymous objects can also be declared for interfaces and abstract classes:

kotlin

```
val clickable = object : OnClickListener {
   override fun onClick() {
      println("Clicked!")
   }
}
```

Nested and inner classes can be declared inside other classes. By default, nested classes are static:

kotlin

```kotlin
class Computer {
    class Keyboard
}
```

To access the outer class context, use inner:

kotlin

```kotlin
class Computer {
    inner class Keyboard {
        fun info() = "Part of ${this@Computer}"
    }
}
```

Common Error Resolution

- Declaring a class without open and trying to inherit from it
  Solution: Add the open modifier when inheritance is needed

- Creating properties with val when changes are required
  Solution: Use var for properties that will be modified during the object's lifecycle

- Omitting init when initialization logic is needed
  Solution: Insert init blocks to execute code right after object creation

- Trying to access this in contexts where inner is not declared
Solution: Mark inner classes with inner when they need to access the parent class

- Using getters/setters with complex logic and no isolation
Solution: Extract logic into private methods when accessors become too complex

Best Practices

- Use the primary constructor whenever possible

- Prefer val over var for properties that don't need to be changed

- Name classes with clear nouns and methods with action verbs

- Declare methods with single expressions for simple behaviors

- Apply object for global configurations and utilities that don't require instantiation

- Create helper functions to encapsulate business rules

- Avoid unnecessary inheritance; prefer composition

- Use sealed to limit known class hierarchies

- Document public class properties and functions

- Split responsibilities into multiple small classes instead of a monolithic one

Strategic Summary

Kotlin's class and object structure provides a solid foundation for system modeling with clarity, safety, and elegance. The use of primary constructors, well-defined properties, concise methods, and init blocks allows for building efficient and scalable object-oriented architectures. By mastering these tools, developers gain the ability to organize code more cohesively, encapsulate business logic precisely, and ensure reuse with technical responsibility.

CHAPTER 8. INHERITANCE AND POLYMORPHISM

Kotlin is a modern language that adopts an explicit and safe approach to inheritance and polymorphism. Unlike languages like Java, where any class can be inherited by default, in Kotlin all classes are final by default. To allow inheritance, the open modifier must be used. This choice reinforces control over the application structure, making extensions more intentional and less likely to cause unintended side effects.

Inheritance allows the creation of a new class based on an existing one, reusing its attributes and methods. Polymorphism enables different classes to handle the same interface or base type differently, while respecting a common contract. Together, these two concepts are fundamental for building extensible, decoupled, and maintainable systems.

Declaring a base class that can be extended requires the open modifier:

kotlin

```kotlin
open class Animal(val name: String) {

    open fun makeSound() {

        println("Generic sound")

    }

}
```

The name property is immutable and initialized in the constructor. The makeSound function is also marked as open, indicating it can be overridden by child classes. To inherit this class, use the colon (:) operator:

kotlin

```kotlin
class Dog(name: String) : Animal(name) {
    override fun makeSound() {
        println("Bark")
    }
}
```

The makeSound function has been overridden using override, and the new behavior will be used when the method is called from a Dog instance:

kotlin

```kotlin
val rex = Dog("Rex")
rex.makeSound() // Bark
```

If the Animal class were not marked as open, the compiler would throw an error, preventing inheritance. This requirement reinforces encapsulation and avoids accidental extensions.

Polymorphism manifests when a reference of the base type stores objects of derived classes:

kotlin

```kotlin
val animal: Animal = Dog("Max")
animal.makeSound() // Bark
```

Even though the declared type is Animal, the method executed is from the Dog instance, thanks to polymorphic behavior. This capability allows writing functions that operate on the base type but execute subclass-specific logic at runtime.

The same principle applies to overridden properties. When a property is declared as open, it can be redefined:

kotlin

```
open class Shape {
    open val sides: Int = 0
}


class Triangle : Shape() {
    override val sides = 3
}
```

Functions can also call the superclass implementation using super:

kotlin

```
open class Instrument {
    open fun play() {
        println("Playing sound")
    }
}


class Guitar : Instrument() {
```

```kotlin
    override fun play() {
        super.play()
        println("Guitar sound")
    }
}
```

Calling super.play() executes the superclass method before applying the additional behavior.

Classes can contain abstract methods or properties using the abstract modifier. This forces subclasses to implement the declared behaviors:

kotlin

```kotlin
abstract class Vehicle {
    abstract fun move()
}
```

Any class that inherits from Vehicle must implement the move function:

kotlin

```kotlin
class Car : Vehicle() {
    override fun move() {
        println("Rolling on four wheels")
    }
}
```

The use of abstract classes is ideal when a common model is

needed, but implementation is delegated to the children. No instances can be created from an abstract class.

The sealed modifier allows limiting the set of subclasses that can inherit from a base class. This restriction makes flow control safer and exhaustive:

kotlin

```
sealed class Result
class Success(val data: String) : Result()
class Error(val message: String) : Result()
```

This structure favors the use of when, ensuring all cases are handled:

kotlin

```
fun process(res: Result) {
    when (res) {
        is Success -> println("Success: ${res.data}")
        is Error -> println("Error: ${res.message}")
    }
}
```

Inheritance also applies to interfaces, with the advantage of allowing multiple implementations:

kotlin

```
interface Clickable {
    fun click()
}
```

```kotlin
class Button : Clickable {
    override fun click() {
        println("Button pressed")
    }
}
```

Interfaces do not contain state, but they can define functions with default implementation:

kotlin

```kotlin
interface Loggable {
    fun log() = println("Event logged")
}
```

A class can inherit from both a class and one or more interfaces, as long as the correct order is respected:

kotlin

```kotlin
class Element : Component(), Clickable, Loggable
```

If two interfaces define methods with the same signature, ambiguity must be resolved explicitly:

kotlin

```kotlin
interface A {
    fun action() = println("Action from A")
}
```

```kotlin
interface B {
    fun action() = println("Action from B")
}


class Implementer : A, B {
    override fun action() {
        super<A>.action()
        super<B>.action()
    }
}
```

Common Error Resolution

- Omitting open when declaring a class or method to be extended
  Solution: Include open to allow inheritance and overriding

- Trying to instantiate an abstract class
  Solution: Create a concrete class that implements the required methods

- Declaring a property with val and trying to override with var
  Solution: Mutability cannot be increased during overriding

- Not covering all possible types in a when with a sealed class
  Solution: Ensure all cases are handled

- Declaring multiple inheritance from classes
  Solution: Kotlin only allows multiple inheritance through interfaces

Best Practices

- Declare classes as final by default and open only when necessary

- Use abstract to define mandatory contracts clearly

- Apply sealed when the set of subclasses is known and closed

- Write override functions with a clear purpose, avoiding duplicate superclass logic

- Favor composition over inheritance in complex structures

- Avoid overlapping responsibilities in derived classes

- Include documentation in base classes to guide correct extension

- Test polymorphic behaviors with base type instances

- Use interfaces to modularize cross-cutting capabilities

- Name inherited classes in a way that clearly reflects their role and extension

Strategic Summary

Inheritance and polymorphism in Kotlin are structured to reinforce conscious design. By requiring open, prohibiting direct multiple class inheritance, and allowing multiple interfaces, the language guides developers toward clearer and safer decisions. By combining abstraction, specialization, and controlled restrictions like sealed, it is possible to create architectures that favor maintainability, extensibility, and testability. Mastering these tools enables the structuring of robust and adaptable systems without sacrificing elegance and technical precision.

CHAPTER 9. INTERFACES AND ABSTRACT CLASSES

Kotlin provides a robust and safe modeling approach for representing shared behaviors and incomplete structures through the use of interfaces and abstract classes. These two features are essential for defining reusable contracts, promoting decoupling between components, and allowing multiple specializations in a clear and intentional way.

Interfaces represent capabilities that a class can implement. They do not hold internal state, only methods that describe behavior. Abstract classes serve as partially implemented models and can contain properties and internal logic. The conscious use of these structures supports the construction of flexible, evolvable, and easier-to-test architectures.

The declaration of an interface is done using the interface keyword:

kotlin

```kotlin
interface Clickable {
    fun click()
}
```

A class can implement the interface and provide concrete behavior:

kotlin

```kotlin
class Button : Clickable {
    override fun click() {
        println("Button pressed")
    }
}
```

Interfaces can also have methods with default implementations:

kotlin

```kotlin
interface Loggable {
    fun log() {
        println("Log recorded")
    }
}
```

When a class implements this interface, it automatically inherits this behavior:

kotlin

```kotlin
class Access : Loggable
```

Instantiating Access and calling log() will execute the interface method. The class may still override this function if custom behavior is needed.

A class can implement multiple interfaces simultaneously:

kotlin

```kotlin
interface Clickable {
    fun click()
```

```
}

interface Draggable {
    fun drag()
}

class Icon : Clickable, Draggable {
    override fun click() {
        println("Icon clicked")
    }

    override fun drag() {
        println("Icon dragged")
    }
}
```

This flexibility makes interfaces ideal for behavior composition, avoiding deep inheritance and promoting greater modularity. Unlike classes, there is no limit to the number of interfaces a class can implement.

In contrast, abstract classes are used when a partially implemented base structure is required. The abstract keyword is used to declare both the class and its required members:

kotlin

```
abstract class Document(val name: String) {
    abstract fun print()
```

```kotlin
    fun save() {
        println("Document $name saved")
    }
}
```

Any class inheriting from Document must implement the print method, but can reuse the save method directly:

kotlin

```kotlin
class Report(name: String) : Document(name) {
    override fun print() {
        println("Printing report $name")
    }
}
```

Unlike interfaces, abstract classes can contain state, property initialization, and complex logic. They also support primary constructors, making it easier to require parameters during subclass creation.

When facing the need to inherit behavior with internal logic and associated data, abstract classes are more appropriate. Interfaces should be used when the intent is only to enforce the presence of methods without defining implementation or state.

When a class implements multiple interfaces with methods of the same signature, conflicts must be resolved explicitly:

kotlin

```kotlin
interface A {
    fun execute() = println("Executing A")
```

```kotlin
}

interface B {
    fun execute() = println("Executing B")
}

class Component : A, B {
    override fun execute() {
        super<A>.execute()
        super<B>.execute()
    }
}
```

This approach gives developers full control over which implementation to use — or whether to combine them.

The language also supports the use of generic interfaces, enabling reusable contracts for different types:

kotlin

```kotlin
interface Storable<T> {
    fun save(item: T)
}
```

This interface can be implemented for any type:

kotlin

```kotlin
class UserRepository : Storable<User> {
```

```
override fun save(item: User) {
    println("User ${item.name} saved")
  }
}
```

This feature is essential in libraries, persistence layers, and domain-driven services.

Common Error Resolution

- Trying to instantiate an interface or abstract class directly
  Solution: Create a concrete implementation that provides the required methods

- Declaring two interfaces with the same function and not resolving the conflict
  Solution: Use super<Interface>.method() to choose which to call

- Using an abstract class without the need for state or internal logic
  Solution: Replace with an interface if the goal is to enforce method signatures only

- Omitting the override modifier when implementing methods
  Solution: Add override for all inherited and customized methods

- Confusing inheritance with multiple implementation
  Solution: Remember that classes inherit from only one

base class, but can implement multiple interfaces

Best Practices

- Use interfaces to define modular and reusable capabilities

- Prefer abstract classes only when there is shared logic or state

- Document interface contracts to guide correct implementations

- Resolve method conflicts clearly, prioritizing readability

- Use descriptive names for interfaces that clearly indicate their purpose (Authenticable, Serializable)

- Avoid deep inheritance — use interface composition instead of complex hierarchies

- Use generic interfaces to create reusable structures across contexts

- Create minimal and testable implementations from well-defined contracts

- Apply the interface segregation principle by avoiding bloated contracts

- Reuse common behaviors in abstract classes only when they are stable and coherent

Strategic Summary

Interfaces and abstract classes are foundational pillars of contract-oriented architecture. By modeling functionality through lean interfaces and base classes with well-defined responsibilities, it's possible to build cohesive, testable, and maintainable systems. Clarity in the boundaries between these two resources allows different parts of a system to evolve independently, preserving technical consistency and supporting extensibility without compromising the robustness of the application.

CHAPTER 10. STRING MANIPULATION

Strings are one of the most used data types in any application. In Kotlin, text manipulation is handled with high expressiveness, safety, and native support for common operations such as interpolation, concatenation, substring extraction, pattern matching, and use of regular expressions. Additionally, the language provides features that make it easier to work with multiline blocks and transformation operations.

A string in Kotlin is represented by the String class, which is immutable. This means that any operation that modifies a string returns a new instance with the updated value, without affecting the original.

String creation is straightforward:

kotlin

```
val message = "Welcome to Kotlin"
```

Interpolation allows variables to be embedded directly within the string using the $ symbol:

kotlin

```
val name = "Carlos"
val greeting = "Hello, $name"
```

You can also interpolate expressions using curly braces:

kotlin

```
val age = 30
val sentence = "Double age: ${age * 2}"
```

This feature improves readability and reduces the need for manual concatenation.

Multiline strings are created with triple double quotes (""") and preserve the text structure, including line breaks:

kotlin

```
val text = """
    Line 1
    Line 2
    Line 3
""".trimIndent()
```

The trimIndent() method removes the common indentation from all lines, making the text visually aligned even within code blocks.

String concatenation can be done with the + operator, although interpolation is preferred for clarity:

kotlin

```
val full = "Name: " + name + ", Age: " + age
```

Kotlin offers various native methods for transforming,

analyzing, and manipulating strings:

- length — returns the length of the string

- uppercase() / lowercase() — converts all characters to uppercase or lowercase

- contains() — checks if the string contains a certain substring

- startsWith() / endsWith() — checks prefix or suffix

- substring() — extracts part of the string

- replace() — replaces segments with other values

- split() — splits the string based on a delimiter

- trim() — removes leading and trailing spaces

- reversed() — reverses the string

- take() / drop() — selects or discards the first characters

- isBlank() / isEmpty() — checks if the string is empty or contains only spaces

Practical usage example:

kotlin

```kotlin
val input = " Kotlin is awesome "
val processed = input.trim().uppercase()
println(processed) // KOTLIN IS AWESOME
```

Regular expressions are fully supported and can be used with the Regex class. A pattern is created as follows:

kotlin

```kotlin
val regex = Regex("[A-Z]{3}[0-9]{4}")
```

This pattern represents three uppercase letters followed by four digits. To check if a string matches the pattern:

kotlin

```kotlin
val code = "ABC1234"
val isValid = regex.matches(code) // true
```

You can also search for matching segments within a text:

kotlin

```kotlin
val text = "Orders: XYZ1234, ABC9876"
val results = regex.findAll(text)
for (result in results) {
    println("Found: ${result.value}")
}
```

To replace segments based on regex:

kotlin

```kotlin
val masked = text.replace(regex, "***REMOVED***")
```

The language also allows combining regex with native functions like filter, map, and groupBy on string collections.

When handling user inputs, file strings, or network messages, it's important to validate the content before performing operations. Functions such as isNotBlank, startsWith, and contains with null checks ensure safety and prevent failures.

Strings are also widely used for formatting values. Kotlin offers direct integration with Java's String.format():

kotlin

val price = 19.99

val formatted = String.format("Price: R$ %.2f", price)

To format dates, numbers, and currency, you can use external libraries such as java.text.NumberFormat or java.time.format.DateTimeFormatter, applying locale-specific formatting in a controlled manner.

In scenarios involving logging, auditing, and building dynamic messages, the clarity of interpolation combined with regex flexibility enables highly functional structures to be built with just a few lines of code.

Common Error Resolution

- Attempting to directly modify a string expecting the original value to change
  Solution: Reassign the result of operations like replace, uppercase, etc., to the variable

- Using split without handling empty elements in poorly formatted input
  Solution: Add filters or validate the number of parts after splitting

- Using regex without properly escaping special characters
  Solution: Check metacharacters used and apply \\ or
  Regex.escape()

- Interpolating complex objects without overriding
  toString()
  Solution: Ensure the class properly implements toString()
  for use in messages

- Ignoring encoding or accents when comparing strings
  from different sources
  Solution: Apply normalization or convert to uppercase/
  lowercase consistently

Best Practices

- Use interpolation instead of concatenation whenever
  possible

- Prefer trimIndent() in multiline strings to maintain clean
  indentation

- Validate string content before applying transformations
  or regex

- Apply replace cautiously, considering usage context and
  potential collisions

- Create reusable regex patterns as constants in utility
  objects

- Document complex regular expressions to ease future
  maintenance

- Specify locale when using region-dependent formatting (numbers, dates, currency)

- Avoid nested substring repetitions — prefer segmented logic

- Analyze user input for invisible characters such as spaces and line breaks

- Standardize text formats in logs, files, and interfaces to simplify future parsing

Strategic Summary

String manipulation in Kotlin combines conciseness with expressive power. With strong support for interpolation, native methods, multiline strings, and regular expressions, developers have a complete set of tools to handle any type of textual content. By applying these tools precisely, it's possible to build input, analysis, and transformation flows that are highly efficient, safe, and readable. Mastering Kotlin's string ecosystem is a decisive step toward building robust solutions in any programming context.

CHAPTER 11. FILE OPERATIONS

Working with files is an essential activity in various applications, especially those requiring data persistence, log reading, content import, or report export. Kotlin, being fully interoperable with the JVM, offers direct access to the standard Java library classes and resources for file and stream manipulation. Additionally, the language provides utility extensions that simplify common operations such as reading, writing, and iteration.

Reading text files can be done with just a few commands using the File class:

kotlin

```
import java.io.File


val content = File("data.txt").readText()
println(content)
```

This method reads the entire file content into a single string. To process it line by line:

kotlin

```
val lines = File("data.txt").readLines()
lines.forEach { println(it) }
```

This approach is ideal for small to medium-sized files. For large files, it's recommended to use buffered reading to avoid loading everything into memory at once.

Writing is also straightforward:

kotlin

```kotlin
File("output.txt").writeText("Output text")
```

This command overwrites any existing content. To append text at the end:

kotlin

```kotlin
File("output.txt").appendText("\nNew line")
```

Kotlin also allows using useLines for efficient processing:

kotlin

```kotlin
File("large.txt").useLines { lines ->
    lines.filter { it.contains("error") }
        .forEach { println(it) }
}
```

This method keeps only one line in memory at a time, avoiding excessive resource consumption.

For binary files, you can work directly with InputStream and OutputStream:

kotlin

```kotlin
val bytes = File("image.png").readBytes()
```

```kotlin
println("Size: ${bytes.size} bytes")
```

Writing binary data:

kotlin

```kotlin
val content = "Text to save".toByteArray()
File("file.bin").writeBytes(content)
```

These operations allow secure handling of images, PDFs, documents, and other non-text formats.

Streams are used for continuous data reading, especially useful when dealing with large volumes. Buffered reading:

kotlin

```kotlin
File("input.log").bufferedReader().use { reader ->
    reader.forEachLine { println(it) }
}
```

Buffered writing:

kotlin

```kotlin
File("output.log").bufferedWriter().use { writer ->
    writer.write("First line\n")
    writer.write("Second line")
}
```

The use function ensures the resource is automatically closed after the operation, preventing memory leaks or locked files in the operating system.

You can work with directories to list files, filter extensions, and create structures:

kotlin

```kotlin
val txtFiles = File("docs").listFiles { _, name ->
    name.endsWith(".txt")
}
txtFiles?.forEach { println(it.name) }
```

Creating directories and files dynamically:

kotlin

```kotlin
val folder = File("reports")
if (!folder.exists()) {
    folder.mkdirs()
}

val newFile = File(folder, "summary.txt")
newFile.writeText("Initial report")
```

For advanced operations such as copying and moving:

kotlin

```kotlin
File("source.txt").copyTo(File("destination.txt"), overwrite = true)
File("destination.txt").delete()
```

These actions should be performed with prior validation to avoid data loss.

When dealing with user input files, uploads, logs, or temporary files, always validate permissions, file existence, and size. Kotlin makes this verification easy:

kotlin

```
val file = File("input.txt")
if (file.exists() && file.canRead()) {
    val content = file.readText()
    println(content)
}
```

Common Error Resolution

- Reading large files with readText and consuming all memory
  Solution: Use useLines or bufferedReader for on-demand reading

- Not closing streams manually and leaving files locked
  Solution: Use use blocks to ensure automatic closure

- Writing files in nonexistent directories
  Solution: Create the directory with mkdirs() before calling writeText

- Accidentally overwriting files with writeText
  Solution: Use appendText or check for existence before overwriting

- Ignoring encoding when reading files with special characters
  Solution: Use readText(Charset.forName("UTF-8")) in cases requiring compatibility

Best Practices

- Use use when handling files and streams to ensure resource release

- Read large files with iterators (useLines, bufferedReader) to optimize memory

- Safely create files and directories by checking for existence

- Validate read/write permissions before manipulating files

- Separate temporary files into controlled directories with periodic cleanup

- Name files clearly to avoid future read collisions

- Use extensions like .txt, .log, .csv according to content

- Handle I/O exceptions with clear and actionable messages

- Apply buffers in sequential writing to improve performance

- Organize files by type or context to ease auditing and maintenance

Strategic Summary

File manipulation in Kotlin combines simplicity and control. With direct access to the Java library and idiomatic Kotlin extensions, robust solutions can be created for reading, writing, and processing files of any size or format. Mastering these operations expands the developer's ability to integrate systems, generate reports, consume external files, and create smart logs. Adopting best practices, validating the environment, and optimizing memory usage are decisive aspects for ensuring stability and efficiency in any application that uses files as input or output data sources.

CHAPTER 12. EXCEPTION HANDLING

Exception handling in Kotlin is designed to provide safety, readability, and full control over error flows. The language takes a modern approach by avoiding mandatory catch blocks like in Java, while still preserving all mechanisms to intercept, handle, and rethrow errors precisely. Conscious use of try, catch, and finally, along with custom exceptions and clear input validation, forms the foundation for stable and resilient applications.

The try block surrounds the code that may throw an exception. When an exception occurs, control is passed to the catch block. After execution, the finally block, if present, will run regardless of success or failure:

kotlin

```kotlin
try {
    val result = 10 / 0
    println("Result: $result")
} catch (e: ArithmeticException) {
    println("Error: division by zero")
} finally {
    println("Operation finalized")
}
```

In this case, the ArithmeticException is caught, preventing the program from terminating abruptly. The finally block executes even after the error, ensuring resource release, connection closure, or audit logs.

You can catch multiple exception types using separate catch blocks or a single block with when:

kotlin

```kotlin
try {
    val list = listOf(1, 2, 3)
    println(list[5])
} catch (e: Exception) {
    when (e) {
        is IndexOutOfBoundsException -> println("Invalid index")
        is NullPointerException -> println("Null value detected")
        else -> println("Unexpected error: ${e.message}")
    }
}
```

Catching specific exceptions is preferable, as it allows more appropriate responses to each failure. Using a generic Exception is acceptable only in security layers, logging, or fallback handling.

Exceptions can be rethrown with throw. This is useful when you want to log the error but allow it to propagate:

kotlin

```kotlin
fun validateEmail(email: String?) {
```

```kotlin
    if (email.isNullOrBlank()) {
        throw IllegalArgumentException("Email cannot be
empty")
    }
}
```

Using custom exceptions improves application semantics:

kotlin

```kotlin
class UserNotFoundException(message: String) :
Exception(message)
```

This exception can be thrown in critical parts of the system:

kotlin

```kotlin
fun findUser(id: Int): User {
    val user = repository.findById(id)
    return user ?: throw UserNotFoundException("User $id not
found")
}
```

When handling exceptions, it's important to never swallow errors silently. An empty catch block harms traceability:

kotlin

```kotlin
// Avoid
catch (e: Exception) {
    // Ignored
}
```

The correct form is to log the error, even if there's no immediate handling:

kotlin

```
catch (e: Exception) {
    println("Captured error: ${e.message}")
}
```

Kotlin also allows using try as an expression. The value of the last executed statement is assigned to a variable:

kotlin

```
val result = try {
    "123".toInt()
} catch (e: NumberFormatException) {
    0
}
```

This reduces the need for branching and supports a more functional, fluent approach.

For light validation flows, conditional expressions are still preferred:

kotlin

```
val age = input.toIntOrNull() ?: throw
IllegalArgumentException("Invalid age")
```

The toIntOrNull() function returns null on conversion

error, avoiding the need for explicit try to catch NumberFormatException.

The language also allows runCatching for encapsulated exception handling:

kotlin

```
val result = runCatching { "abc".toInt() }

    .onSuccess { println("Converted value: $it") }

    .onFailure { println("Conversion failed: ${it.message}") }
```

This pattern is useful in structures requiring pipelines or chained lambdas, such as reactive operators or fallback chains.

Exceptions should not be used as a control flow tool. Preventive validations using if, require, check, assert, and nullability checks reduce the need to capture avoidable errors:

kotlin

```
val name = requireNotNull(input) { "Name is required" }
```

This command throws an IllegalArgumentException with a custom message if the value is null.

Creating validation layers, filters, and interceptors that handle exceptions in a standardized way contributes to system consistency. In APIs, for example, errors can be centralized in middleware that returns friendly user messages while maintaining complete technical logs.

Common Error Resolution

- Catching generic Exception and ignoring the cause

Solution: Log the error or convert it into a controlled response

- Using exceptions to divert expected flow
Solution: Validate values with if, require, check, or toXOrNull when possible

- Reusing files, connections, or data after failure without revalidating state
Solution: Close and reinitialize resources before retrying operations

- Throwing exceptions with vague or generic messages
Solution: Use clear and specific messages with error context

- Using finally for business logic, compromising the flow
Solution: Reserve finally only for resource release

Best Practices

- Catch specific exceptions whenever possible

- Create custom exceptions with descriptive names

- Use try as an expression to safely return values

- Log all unexpected failures, even if not handled immediately

- Avoid nested try-catch blocks — isolate failures in smaller functions

- Use runCatching, toXOrNull, require, check for validation

without catching

- Centralize exception handling in application layers (services, controllers)

- Define business rules with specific and coherent messages

- Distinguish business failures (like validation) from technical failures (like I/O, network)

- Isolate error recovery in functions with clear reprocessing or fallback

Strategic Summary

Exception handling in Kotlin is flexible, efficient, and strongly oriented toward safety. By mastering capture techniques, rethrowing, early validation, and error customization, developers strengthen system robustness and predictability. Errors should be handled with clarity and intentionality, promoting an architecture where failures are expected, diagnosable, and resolved in a structured manner. The combination of features like try, catch, finally, require, runCatching, and custom exceptions provides a complete foundation for secure, resilient, and technically mature applications.

CHAPTER 13. OBJECT-ORIENTED PROGRAMMING

Object-oriented programming is one of the most established paradigms in software development. In Kotlin, the pillars of this paradigm are preserved with clarity and reinforced by a concise, safe, and modern syntax. Encapsulation, inheritance, polymorphism, and abstraction are implemented through explicit and flexible mechanisms that benefit both beginner developers and architects of complex systems.

The object-oriented paradigm organizes software around entities called objects, which represent elements of the real world or a logical domain. Each object is an instance of a class, containing attributes (properties) and behaviors (methods). Kotlin treats these concepts with simplicity, without sacrificing the technical depth required.

Encapsulation is the practice of protecting an object's internal data, allowing its state to be accessed or modified only through controlled means. Kotlin applies encapsulation by default with visibility modifiers and properties managed via val, var, and custom accessors:

kotlin

```kotlin
class BankAccount {
    private var balance: Double = 0.0

    fun deposit(amount: Double) {
```

```
    if (amount > 0) balance += amount

  }


  fun getBalance(): Double {

    return balance

  }

}
```

The balance attribute is encapsulated and cannot be accessed directly from outside the class. The deposit and getBalance operations offer a secure usage interface, ensuring state integrity.

In addition to private, Kotlin allows the modifiers protected, internal, and public. The default is public, but more restrictive scopes are recommended whenever possible.

Inheritance allows a class to share behaviors with others, promoting reuse and hierarchical organization. In Kotlin, classes are final by default. To allow inheritance, the open modifier must be used:

kotlin

```
open class Person(val name: String) {

  open fun speak() {

    println("Speaking as a person")

  }

}


class Teacher(name: String) : Person(name) {
```

```kotlin
override fun speak() {

    println("Giving a lecture")

}

}
```

The Teacher class inherits from Person and overrides the speak method, illustrating the use of the override modifier to indicate a behavior is being changed.

Polymorphism allows the same method to have different behaviors depending on the object type invoking it. This is possible because base-type references can point to subclass objects:

kotlin

```kotlin
fun introduce(person: Person) {

    person.speak()

}
```

If introduce is called with a Teacher instance, the overridden method will execute. This flexibility allows decoupling code and working with heterogeneous collections elegantly:

kotlin

```kotlin
val people: List<Person> = listOf(Person("Ana"),
Teacher("Carlos"))

people.forEach { it.speak() }
```

Abstraction is achieved through abstract classes and interfaces. Abstract classes can contain partial implementations, while interfaces define only contracts:

kotlin

```
abstract class Document(val title: String) {

    abstract fun print()

}


class Report(title: String) : Document(title) {

    override fun print() {

        println("Printing report: $title")

    }

}
```

Interfaces, in turn, define behavior without worrying about implementation:

kotlin

```
interface Authenticable {

    fun authenticate(password: String): Boolean

}
```

A class can inherit a single superclass, but can implement multiple interfaces:

kotlin

```
class User(val name: String, private val password: String) :
Authenticable {

    override fun authenticate(password: String): Boolean =
this.password == password

}
```

Kotlin also allows object-oriented design patterns to be applied naturally. A commonly used pattern is the **Factory Method**:

kotlin

```kotlin
interface Shape {
    fun draw()
}


class Circle : Shape {
    override fun draw() = println("Drawing a circle")
}


class Rectangle : Shape {
    override fun draw() = println("Drawing a rectangle")
}


object ShapeFactory {
    fun create(type: String): Shape = when (type) {
        "circle" -> Circle()
        "rectangle" -> Rectangle()
        else -> throw IllegalArgumentException("Unknown type")
    }
}
```

Using object to declare ShapeFactory **guarantees a single shared** instance, applying the Singleton pattern.

Another common pattern is **Strategy**, which allows changing a class's behavior at runtime:

kotlin

```kotlin
interface Sorting {
    fun sort(list: List<Int>): List<Int>
}


class Ascending : Sorting {
    override fun sort(list: List<Int>) = list.sorted()
}


class Descending : Sorting {
    override fun sort(list: List<Int>) = list.sortedDescending()
}


class Sorter(private var strategy: Sorting) {
    fun sort(list: List<Int>) = strategy.sort(list)
    fun setStrategy(new: Sorting) {
        strategy = new
    }
}
```

Encapsulating strategies allows the sorting behavior to be changed without modifying the structure of the Sorter object.

Kotlin encourages a modern object-oriented approach focused

on clean code and behavior composition. Instead of deep inheritance, it's preferable to use small interfaces, delegation, and scope functions to promote reuse without excessive coupling.

Common Error Resolution

- Forgetting to declare open on classes or methods meant to be inherited
  Solution: Add open explicitly to allow extension

- Applying inheritance where composition would be more appropriate
  Solution: Evaluate whether the class is a true subtype or merely shares functionality

- Not encapsulating sensitive or mutable attributes
  Solution: Use private and provide controlled public methods

- Implementing large interfaces with unused methods
  Solution: Split interfaces into smaller contracts with single responsibilities

- Ignoring the use of override in inherited methods
  Solution: Explicitly declare overrides to avoid ambiguity and logic errors

Best Practices

- Use composition over inheritance whenever possible

- Declare attributes with val to reinforce immutability

- Modularize behavior with small, reusable interfaces

- Create methods with well-defined responsibilities and descriptive names

- Apply visibility modifiers to protect internal class state

- Clearly document contracts in public interfaces

- Use abstract classes only when there is shared logic to inherit

- Avoid circular dependencies between classes

- Follow the Single Responsibility Principle (SRP) for each class

- Prioritize clarity over premature optimization when structuring hierarchies

Strategic Summary

Object-oriented programming in Kotlin is implemented with elegance and control. The language provides all the classic mechanisms of the paradigm, along with additional tools that promote readability, modularization, and clean design. By applying encapsulation, inheritance, polymorphism, and abstraction in a structured way, developers build systems that are more robust, flexible, and ready to evolve with stability. Mastering these pillars is decisive for turning requirements into well-defined, organized, and scalable architectures.

CHAPTER 14. FUNCTIONAL PROGRAMMING

Kotlin incorporates the main concepts of functional programming without abandoning object-oriented principles. The language treats functions as first-class objects, promotes immutability, allows functional composition, and offers powerful operators such as map, filter, fold, and reduce. With this hybrid approach, developers have access to features that increase expressiveness, reduce side effects, and promote clean, predictable, and modular code.

Functions as First-Class Objects mean that functions can be assigned to variables, passed as parameters, returned from other functions, and stored in collections. This enables abstraction of behavior in a reusable way:

kotlin

```
val greeting: (String) -> String = { name -> "Hello, $name" }
println(greeting("Kotlin"))
```

The variable greeting holds a function that takes a String and returns another String. This flexibility enables the construction of execution pipelines with interchangeable logic.

Functions can also be passed as arguments:

kotlin

```
fun applyOperation(x: Int, operation: (Int) -> Int): Int {
```

```
    return operation(x)
}
```

```
val double = { it: Int -> it * 2 }
val result = applyOperation(5, double) // 10
```

This pattern is useful when behavior needs to be defined outside the main function, promoting decoupling and modularity.

Functional Composition allows functions to be chained so that the result of one becomes the input of the next. In Kotlin, this can be done explicitly:

kotlin

```
fun add5(x: Int) = x + 5
fun double(x: Int) = x * 2
```

```
val composed = { x: Int -> double(add5(x)) }
println(composed(3)) // 16
```

Although Kotlin doesn't provide native composition operators (compose, andThen), it's possible to create extensions to facilitate this pattern:

kotlin

```
infix fun <P1, R, R2> ((P1) -> R).then(f: (R) -> R2): (P1) -> R2 =
{ p1 -> f(this(p1)) }
```

```kotlin
val pipeline = ::add5 then ::double
println(pipeline(3)) // 16
```

Immutability is one of the pillars of functional programming. Variables declared with val cannot be reassigned. This ensures predictability and avoids hard-to-track side effects:

kotlin

```kotlin
val numbers = listOf(1, 2, 3)
val doubled = numbers.map { it * 2 }
```

The original collection remains unchanged. All transformations create new structures, making application state easier to trace.

Functional Operators like map, filter, fold, and reduce are widely used to transform data:

kotlin

```kotlin
val list = listOf(1, 2, 3, 4, 5)

val evens = list.filter { it % 2 == 0 }        // [2, 4]
val squares = list.map { it * it }          // [1, 4, 9, 16, 25]
val sum = list.reduce { acc, value -> acc + value } // 15
val accumulated = list.fold(10) { acc, value -> acc + value } // 25
```

reduce aggregates list values using the first element as the accumulator. fold starts with an arbitrary initial value, useful when a base not present in the list is needed.

Using fold can be extended to more complex transformations:

kotlin

```
val text = listOf("kotlin", "is", "functional")

val result = text.fold("") { acc, word -> "$acc $
{word.uppercase()}" }.trim()
```

This technique avoids explicit loops and builds readable pipelines.

The flatMap function applies a transformation and "flattens" the results:

kotlin

```
val data = listOf("a,b", "c,d")

val combined = data.flatMap { it.split(",") } // ["a", "b", "c", "d"]
```

groupBy allows grouping data based on a derived key:

kotlin

```
val names = listOf("Ana", "Amanda", "Carlos", "Camila")

val grouped = names.groupBy { it.first() } // map of A -> [Ana,
Amanda], C -> [Carlos, Camila]
```

Functional programming also promotes the absence of side effects. Functions should operate only on their inputs, without modifying external variables or relying on mutable state:

kotlin

```
fun square(x: Int): Int = x * x
```

This function is pure: given the same input, it always returns the same output, without altering anything in the external environment.

Lambdas using it allow even more compact anonymous functions:

kotlin

```
val reversed = listOf("Kotlin", "Java").map { it.reversed() }
```

When the context is clear, this kind of expression is easy to read and eliminates the need for temporary names.

Scope Functions like run, let, apply, also, and with also reflect functional programming principles by encapsulating context, applying transformations, and returning values in a controlled way:

kotlin

```
val result = "kotlin"
    .let { it.uppercase() }
    .run { "Result: $this" }
```

Common Error Resolution

- Using mutable variables in functional operations
  Solution: Use val and avoid mutation inside lambdas

- Creating long lambdas with multiple responsibilities
  Solution: Extract logic into named helper functions

- Using reduce without ensuring the collection is not empty

Solution: Check content or use fold with an initial value

- Confusing flatMap with map and generating nested lists
  Solution: Use flatMap when the transformation returns lists

- Nesting multiple map and filter without readability
  Solution: Split pipeline into named steps

Best Practices

- Treat functions as values — store, pass, and return functions whenever useful

- Use pure functions and immutability for predictability

- Compose small functions with single responsibilities

- Use fold for aggregations with safe initial values

- Apply flatMap and groupBy to transform structured collections

- Name complex lambdas or extract them as functions to maintain clarity

- Avoid modifications outside functional scope

- Prefer val over var in all data structures

- Separate long pipelines into readable intermediate blocks

- Document reusable and pure functions with well-defined inputs and outputs

Strategic Summary

Functional programming in Kotlin extends the expressive capabilities of the language without compromising readability. The use of functions as first-class objects, declarative operators, composition, and immutability allows for the construction of concise, robust, and maintainable solutions. By adopting this paradigm, developers reduce side effects, simplify testing, promote reuse, and enhance the technical quality of the system. Mastering functional techniques in Kotlin is a strategic advantage for any project seeking clarity, safety, and performance in handling data and behaviors.

CHAPTER 15. ASYNCHRONOUS PROGRAMMING WITH COROUTINES

Asynchronous programming is essential for building modern, responsive, and scalable applications. Kotlin offers a native and powerful solution for handling concurrency through the use of coroutines. Support is provided by the kotlinx.coroutines library, which simplifies the development of parallel and non-blocking tasks without sacrificing code readability or sequential logic.

Coroutines are lightweight constructs that allow suspending and resuming function execution without blocking the main thread. They replace traditional patterns like callbacks and promises, enabling asynchronous code to be written with the same structure as synchronous code.

To use coroutines, include the dependency:

kotlin

```
implementation("org.jetbrains.kotlinx:kotlinx-coroutines-core:1.7.3")
```

The entry point for starting a coroutine is the launch function, which starts a new routine asynchronously:

kotlin

```
import kotlinx.coroutines.*
```

```kotlin
fun main() = runBlocking {
    launch {
        delay(1000)
        println("Executed after 1 second")
    }
    println("Start")
}
```

The runBlocking function creates an execution scope that blocks the thread until all coroutines launched within it are finished. It is useful only in environments like main() or tests. In real applications, runBlocking should be replaced with non-blocking scopes such as GlobalScope, CoroutineScope, or lifecycle-aware scopes in specific frameworks.

The delay function suspends coroutine execution without blocking the thread. This behavior is essential for freeing up resources while waiting for external responses such as API calls, disk access, or database queries.

In addition to launch, you can use async to start a coroutine that returns a value. The result is accessed via await:

kotlin

```kotlin
fun main() = runBlocking {
    val result = async {
        delay(500)
        42
    }
    println("Received value: ${result.await()}")
```

```
}
```

Unlike launch, which returns a Job, async returns a Deferred<T>, allowing it to be used like a future. This pattern is useful for parallelizing calls that must complete before continuing the main flow.

With withContext, you can dynamically change the dispatcher of a coroutine, directing its execution to a different context. Common dispatchers include:

- Dispatchers.Default: ideal for CPU-intensive operations

- Dispatchers.IO: optimized for I/O operations such as file reading or network calls

- Dispatchers.Main: used for graphical interfaces such as Android

- Dispatchers.Unconfined: executes immediately in the current thread until the first suspension

kotlin

```kotlin
suspend fun loadData(): String = withContext(Dispatchers.IO) {
    delay(1000)
    "Data loaded"
}
```

The function above runs in a pool optimized for I/O tasks, freeing the main thread and ensuring efficiency.

Coroutines can be organized into scopes for lifecycle control and coordinated cancellation. A scope allows multiple tasks to be launched simultaneously and canceled together:

kotlin

```kotlin
val scope = CoroutineScope(Dispatchers.Default)


val job = scope.launch {
    repeat(5) {
        delay(500)
        println("Processing $it")
    }
}


Thread.sleep(1200)
job.cancel() // Cancels execution
```

Coroutines support cooperative cancellation. This means the task must periodically check if it should continue. The isActive function allows this check:

kotlin

```kotlin
launch {
    for (i in 1..10) {
        if (!isActive) break
        println("Item $i")
        delay(100)
    }
}
```

When a coroutine is canceled, it throws a CancellationException. **To capture or finish cleanly, use** try-finally:

kotlin

```kotlin
val job = launch {
    try {
        repeat(100) {
            println("Operation $it")
            delay(50)
        }
    } finally {
        println("Clean finalization")
    }
}
delay(500)
job.cancelAndJoin()
```

For applications requiring real parallelism, you can launch several coroutines with async **and await all with** awaitAll:

kotlin

```kotlin
val time = measureTimeMillis {
    val one = async { slowTask1() }
    val two = async { slowTask2() }
    println("Result: ${one.await() + two.await()}")
}
```

This pattern improves overall performance when independent tasks can be executed in parallel. The use of measureTimeMillis helps evaluate actual performance gains.

Coroutines can also handle exceptions in a controlled manner. Use CoroutineExceptionHandler for that:

kotlin

```
val handler = CoroutineExceptionHandler { _, ex ->
    println("Error caught: ${ex.message}")
}


val job = CoroutineScope(Dispatchers.Default).launch(handler) {
    throw RuntimeException("Unexpected failure")
}
```

This pattern prevents silent errors from breaking the application or causing unpredictable behavior.

Common Error Resolution

- Using runBlocking in non-blocking environments like Android
  Solution: Use appropriate scopes with launch and async

- Forgetting to call await() in async calls
  Solution: Always retrieve the value with await to ensure execution

- Blocking the main thread with Thread.sleep() inside a coroutine

Solution: Replace with delay to ensure suspension without blocking

- Executing I/O operations in Dispatchers.Default
  Solution: Use Dispatchers.IO for file, network, and database access

- Ignoring cancellation and continuing execution after cancel()
  Solution: Check isActive or use ensureActive() in long loops

Best Practices

- Use launch for fire-and-forget tasks and async for result-producing tasks

- Apply withContext to isolate I/O and CPU loads in appropriate threads

- Keep coroutines short, focused, and decoupled

- Explicitly cancel Jobs when the scope is finished

- Chain async calls with awaitAll to maximize parallelism

- Use supervisorScope when one failure should not cancel sibling coroutines

- Centralize error handling with CoroutineExceptionHandler

- Use measureTimeMillis to evaluate real performance improvements

- Control scope visibility, avoiding GlobalScope except for truly global tasks

- Test asynchronous routines with tools like runTest from kotlinx-coroutines-test

Strategic Summary

Asynchronous programming with coroutines in Kotlin provides a clear, safe, and high-performance approach to handling concurrency and parallelism. By moving away from callback-based and manually threaded models, developers can write sequential-looking code that behaves asynchronously and efficiently. Mastering tools like launch, async, await, withContext, and proper usage of Dispatchers enables the creation of reactive, responsive, and scalable systems ready to meet the demands of modern applications.

CHAPTER 16. REST API INTEGRATION

Integrating with REST APIs is a common requirement in modern applications. Kotlin provides robust, idiomatic, and highly efficient solutions for consuming external services, performing HTTP requests, handling JSON, and processing responses in a safe and asynchronous manner. The two most commonly used approaches in the language are **Retrofit**, popular in Android applications, and **Ktor**, an asynchronous and multiplatform framework ideal for both clients and servers.

Retrofit is a library developed by Square that simplifies REST calls using method annotations and automatic data serialization. To use it, add the dependencies to your build.gradle.kts:

kotlin

```
implementation("com.squareup.retrofit2:retrofit:2.9.0")

implementation("com.squareup.retrofit2:converter-gson:2.9.0")
```

Define an interface representing the API:

kotlin

```
interface ApiService {
    @GET("usuarios")
    suspend fun listUsers(): List<User>
```

```kotlin
@POST("login")
    suspend fun authenticate(@Body credentials: Credentials): Token
}
```

The @GET and @POST annotations define the request type, and the suspend modifier allows asynchronous execution with coroutines. Data models can be represented with simple classes:

kotlin

```kotlin
data class User(val id: Int, val name: String)

data class Credentials(val username: String, val password: String)

data class Token(val token: String)
```

Create the service instance:

kotlin

```kotlin
val retrofit = Retrofit.Builder()
    .baseUrl("https://api.myservice.com/")
    .addConverterFactory(GsonConverterFactory.create())
    .build()

val api = retrofit.create(ApiService::class.java)
```

Consume the API with a coroutine:

kotlin

```kotlin
val users = api.listUsers()
users.forEach { println(it.name) }
```

Authentication can be handled with custom headers. Retrofit allows adding interceptors to include the token in each request:

kotlin

```kotlin
val client = OkHttpClient.Builder()
    .addInterceptor { chain ->
        val request = chain.request().newBuilder()
            .addHeader("Authorization", "Bearer $token")
            .build()
        chain.proceed(request)
    }.build()

val retrofitAuth = Retrofit.Builder()
    .baseUrl("https://api.secure.com/")
    .client(client)
    .addConverterFactory(GsonConverterFactory.create())
    .build()
```

This centralizes authentication logic and allows reuse across all API calls.

JSON processing is done via Gson or Moshi, automatically converting between Kotlin objects and JSON structures. For specific mappings, custom adapters or annotations can be used.

Ktor is a native asynchronous alternative for HTTP clients in Kotlin. It provides more control, multiplatform support, and direct integration with coroutines.

Add dependencies:

kotlin

```
implementation("io.ktor:ktor-client-core:2.3.1")

implementation("io.ktor:ktor-client-cio:2.3.1")

implementation("io.ktor:ktor-client-content-
negotiation:2.3.1")

implementation("io.ktor:ktor-serialization-gson:2.3.1")
```

Create a Ktor client with JSON support:

kotlin

```
val client = HttpClient(CIO) {
    install(ContentNegotiation) {
        gson()
    }
}
```

Make a GET request:

kotlin

```
val users: List<User> = client.get("https://api.kotlinktor.dev/
users").body()
```

Make a POST request with a body:

kotlin

```
val response: Token = client.post("https://api.kotlinktor.dev/
login") {

    contentType(ContentType.Application.Json)

    setBody(Credentials("admin", "123456"))
}.body()
```

Authentication with token can be configured with default headers:

kotlin

```
val client = HttpClient(CIO) {

    install(ContentNegotiation) {

        gson()

    }

    defaultRequest {

        header("Authorization", "Bearer $token")

    }

}
```

Both libraries support cancellation via CoroutineScope, error handling with try-catch, and long operations with withTimeout.

HTTP Error Handling should consider status codes, network exceptions, and serialization errors:

kotlin

```
try {

    val response = api.listUsers()
```

```
    println("Success: ${response.size} users")
} catch (e: HttpException) {
    println("HTTP Error: ${e.code()}")
} catch (e: IOException) {
    println("Connection failure: ${e.message}")
}
```

In scalable applications, it's recommended to create **repository layers** that encapsulate network logic and expose only processed data. This separates presentation logic and enables reuse across multiple application components.

Common Error Resolution

- Forgetting to mark Retrofit methods with suspend
  Solution: Add suspend to enable coroutine-based async calls

- Ignoring HTTP error handling with try-catch
  Solution: Catch HttpException and IOException separately for precise diagnostics

- Trying to consume API responses without configuring ConverterFactory or Ktor serialization
  Solution: Add GsonConverterFactory or install(ContentNegotiation)

- Misconfiguring base URL in Retrofit without trailing slash
  Solution: Ensure the base URL ends with / to avoid endpoint composition errors

- Using GlobalScope for async calls without lifecycle control

Solution: Use appropriate scopes like CoroutineScope or lifecycleScope (Android)

Best Practices

- Define simple and clear data models to simplify serialization

- Centralize authentication configuration using interceptors or defaultRequest

- Separate network logic into reusable layers (API + Repository)

- Use withTimeout to avoid indefinitely pending calls

- Validate deserialized data before usage

- Map error codes into user-friendly messages

- Use detailed logs for requests and responses during development

- Reduce coupling between network and UI components via interfaces

- Mock responses in tests to avoid network dependency

- Configure custom serializers for optional fields or specific formats

Strategic Summary

REST API integration in Kotlin is empowered by mature tools designed to align with the language's asynchronous paradigm. Using **Retrofit** or **Ktor**, developers can consume external services with security, fluidity, and high performance. The combination of coroutines, structured error handling, and automatic serialization enables the creation of modern, reactive, and highly testable applications. By mastering these techniques, developers elevate the level of interoperability, connectivity, and reliability in their systems, with full control over client-server data flows.

CHAPTER 17. DATA PERSISTENCE

Data persistence is a core pillar for applications that need to maintain state between sessions, store user information, synchronize content with servers, or ensure the integrity of critical operations. In Kotlin, working with relational databases is made seamless by **SQLite**, a lightweight embedded file-based database, and **Room**, a modern and secure abstraction library built specifically for use with SQLite. This combination provides complete CRUD operations, support for optimized SQL queries, and native relationship management between entities.

SQLite is a file-based local database. It's widely used in Android and embedded environments due to its lightweight nature, reliability, and easy integration. While it's possible to use the SQLiteOpenHelper class directly, the recommended way is via **Room**, which offers:

- Coroutine support

- Compile-time validation

- Direct use of Kotlin data classes

Setting Up Room

Add the dependencies:

kotlin

```
implementation("androidx.room:room-runtime:2.5.2")
kapt("androidx.room:room-compiler:2.5.2")
```

```
implementation("androidx.room:room-ktx:2.5.2")
```

Define an **Entity**, which represents a database table:

kotlin

```
@Entity(tableName = "usuarios")
data class Usuario(
    @PrimaryKey(autoGenerate = true) val id: Int = 0,
    val nome: String,
    val email: String
)
```

Each property becomes a table column. @PrimaryKey defines the primary key, and autoGenerate automatically handles ID generation.

Define the **DAO (Data Access Object)** interface, responsible for database operations:

kotlin

```
@Dao
interface UsuarioDao {
    @Insert
    suspend fun inserir(usuario: Usuario)

    @Update
    suspend fun atualizar(usuario: Usuario)

    @Delete
```

```kotlin
    suspend fun remover(usuario: Usuario)


    @Query("SELECT * FROM usuarios")
    suspend fun listarTodos(): List<Usuario>


    @Query("SELECT * FROM usuarios WHERE email = :email")
    suspend fun buscarPorEmail(email: String): Usuario?
}
```

These functions represent the CRUD operations: Create, Read, Update, and Delete. The use of suspend allows seamless integration with coroutines for non-blocking asynchronous operations.

Configure the **database class** extending RoomDatabase:

kotlin

```kotlin
@Database(entities = [Usuario::class], version = 1)
abstract class AppDatabase : RoomDatabase() {
    abstract fun usuarioDao(): UsuarioDao
}
```

Create the **singleton instance** of the database:

kotlin

```kotlin
val db = Room.databaseBuilder(
    context,
    AppDatabase::class.java, "meu-banco.db"
).build()
```

```kotlin
val dao = db.usuarioDao()
```

Performing operations:

kotlin

```kotlin
val novoUsuario = Usuario(nome = "Carlos", email = "carlos@email.com")
dao.inserir(novoUsuario)
```

```kotlin
val usuarios = dao.listarTodos()
usuarios.forEach { println(it.nome) }
```

Updates and deletions are done using the full object. Room automatically tracks entity fields and applies the necessary changes.

Advanced Queries use SQL operators like LIKE, IN, BETWEEN, ORDER BY, LIMIT, and subqueries:

kotlin

```kotlin
@Query("SELECT * FROM usuarios WHERE nome LIKE :prefixo || '%' ORDER BY nome ASC LIMIT 10")
suspend fun buscarPorPrefixo(prefixo: String): List<Usuario>
```

Reactive Queries can be exposed using Flow, integrating with LiveData or StateFlow:

kotlin

```kotlin
@Query("SELECT * FROM usuarios")
```

```kotlin
fun observarUsuarios(): Flow<List<Usuario>>
```

This is useful in UI layers where live updates are required.

Entity Relationships such as 1:N or N:N can be handled using @Relation:

kotlin

```kotlin
@Entity
data class Usuario(
    @PrimaryKey val id: Int,
    val nome: String
)


@Entity
data class Pedido(
    @PrimaryKey val id: Int,
    val usuarioId: Int,
    val descricao: String
)


data class UsuarioComPedidos(
    @Embedded val usuario: Usuario,
    @Relation(
        parentColumn = "id",
        entityColumn = "usuarioId"
```

```
)
    val pedidos: List<Pedido>
)
```

Return this composite structure in DAO:

kotlin

```
@Transaction
@Query("SELECT * FROM Usuario")
suspend fun listarComPedidos(): List<UsuarioComPedidos>
```

This enables grouped and structured queries, improving performance by reducing multiple database calls.

Common Error Resolution

- Using the same field name in multiple entities without @Embedded or @ColumnInfo
  Solution: Apply @Embedded properly or rename columns using @ColumnInfo

- Forgetting to mark DAO methods with suspend
  Solution: Add suspend to all database access functions

- Returning unsupported types without converters
  Solution: Create @TypeConverter for complex types like Date, List, Enum

- Ignoring concurrency exceptions from duplicate inserts
  Solution: Use @Insert(onConflict = OnConflictStrategy.REPLACE) or define conflict policy

- Leaving database instances unmanaged
  Solution: Use a singleton instance scoped to the application lifecycle

Best Practices

- Use RoomDatabase as a singleton to prevent multiple open connections

- Organize files into layers (entity, DAO, database) for better structure

- Declare all SQL queries in DAO — avoid raw SQL in other parts of the code

- Use Flow for data that needs to be observed continuously

- Validate data before persisting to avoid inconsistency

- Document SQL queries in the DAO for maintainability

- Apply @Transaction to methods that perform multiple atomic operations

- Use @Index for frequently used columns in WHERE or JOIN

- Write unit tests for DAOs using in-memory databases (Room.inMemoryDatabaseBuilder)

- Avoid direct access to the database outside DAO to maintain separation of concerns

Strategic Summary

Data persistence with SQLite and Room in Kotlin offers a reliable, secure, and highly integrated solution within the Kotlin ecosystem. The use of immutable data models, coroutine-based asynchronous operations, and expressive queries with compile-time safety creates a solid foundation for robust and scalable applications. By mastering entity structures, DAOs, relationships, and reactive flows, developers gain full control over the data layer, ensuring the integrity and consistency of information in any usage scenario.

CHAPTER 18. AUTOMATED TESTING WITH KOTLIN

Automated testing is fundamental for ensuring the reliability, stability, and maintainability of any application. In Kotlin, native support for unit testing, integration testing, and mocking is solid, backed by widely adopted libraries such as **JUnit 5** and **MockK**. This combination allows developers to validate functionality at different levels, avoid regressions, and continuously improve code quality with confidence.

JUnit 5 is the standard testing framework for Kotlin on the JVM. It offers features such as test annotations, parameterized execution, grouping, ordering, and behavior customization. **MockK** is the most recommended library for creating mock objects in Kotlin, allowing developers to isolate dependencies during testing and accurately validate interactions.

Setting Up

Add the following dependencies to your build.gradle.kts:

kotlin

```
testImplementation("org.junit.jupiter:junit-jupiter:5.10.0")

testImplementation("io.mockk:mockk:1.13.8")

testImplementation("org.jetbrains.kotlinx:kotlinx-coroutines-test:1.7.3")
```

Basic Unit Test with JUnit 5

kotlin

```kotlin
import org.junit.jupiter.api.Assertions.*
import org.junit.jupiter.api.Test

class CalculatorTest {
    @Test
    fun `should correctly sum two numbers`() {
        val result = Calculator().sum(3, 5)
        assertEquals(8, result)
    }
}

class Calculator {
    fun sum(a: Int, b: Int): Int = a + b
}
```

Method names should be descriptive, preferably formatted as sentences to clearly explain the expected behavior. This improves test report readability and helps document business rules.

Using MockK for Dependency Isolation

kotlin

```kotlin
import io.mockk.every
import io.mockk.mockk
import org.junit.jupiter.api.Test
import kotlin.test.assertEquals
```

```kotlin
class UserServiceTest {
    private val repository = mockk<UserRepository>()
    private val service = UserService(repository)

    @Test
    fun `should return user name when fetched by ID`() {
        every { repository.findById(1) } returns User(1, "Carlos")

        val result = service.getUserName(1)

        assertEquals("Carlos", result)
    }
}
```

To verify interactions:

kotlin

```kotlin
import io.mockk.verify


verify { repository.findById(1) }
```

To simulate failures:

kotlin

```kotlin
every { repository.findById(999) } throws
UserNotFoundException("User not found")
```

Testing Asynchronous Code with Coroutines

Use runTest from kotlinx-coroutines-test to test suspend functions:

kotlin

```
import kotlinx.coroutines.test.runTest


@Test
fun `should return correct value after async execution`() =
runTest {
    val result = myClass.suspendFunction()
    assertEquals("value", result)
}
```

This approach executes suspend functions in a controlled environment without blocking the main thread. It also allows control over virtual time for testing delays and timeouts.

Integration Testing

Integration tests validate the interaction between components using real instances. For example, Room allows testing with an in-memory database:

kotlin

```
val db = Room.inMemoryDatabaseBuilder(
    context,
    AppDatabase::class.java
).build()
```

Unit tests (fast, isolated) and integration tests (slower, real resources) should be clearly separated, both by folders and naming conventions.

Parameterized Tests

JUnit 5 supports parameterized execution:

kotlin

```kotlin
import org.junit.jupiter.params.ParameterizedTest
import org.junit.jupiter.params.provider.CsvSource


@ParameterizedTest
@CsvSource(
    "2,3,5",
    "10,5,15"
)
fun `should sum various number pairs`(a: Int, b: Int, expected: Int) {
    val result = Calculator().sum(a, b)
    assertEquals(expected, result)
}
```

This increases coverage with less repetition.

Lifecycle Hooks

Use lifecycle annotations to setup and teardown resources:

kotlin

```kotlin
@BeforeEach
fun setup() {
    service = UserService(mockk())
}
```

Useful Assertions

- assertEquals – compares values

- assertTrue, assertFalse – boolean checks

- assertThrows – ensures an exception is thrown

- assertNotNull – confirms a value is not null

Custom assertions improve clarity and reuse:

kotlin

```kotlin
fun assertUserIsActive(user: User) {
    assertTrue(user.isActive)
    assertNotNull(user.activationDate)
}
```

Common Error Resolution

- Failing to isolate real dependencies in unit tests
  Solution: Use MockK to simulate external behavior

- Testing multiple responsibilities in a single test
  Solution: Split into smaller, focused tests

- Ignoring expected exceptions
  Solution: Use assertThrows to validate errors

- Tests depending on execution order
  Solution: Make each test independent with its own data

- Testing only success flows
  Solution: Add test cases for errors, edge cases, and invalid input

Best Practices

- Write unit tests for pure functions and business logic

- Use mocks only for external dependencies

- Create descriptive test names that reflect expected behavior

- Organize tests into folders that mirror the production structure

- Clearly separate unit and integration tests

- Cover both positive and negative flows for each critical function

- Use runTest for suspending functions and control virtual time

- Use in-memory databases or local services in integration

tests

- Automate test execution in CI/CD to ensure zero regression

- Reassess failing tests regularly — they should reveal real problems, not noise

Strategic Summary

Automated testing in Kotlin is supported by mature and highly integrated tools. The combination of JUnit 5, MockK, and coroutine testing utilities enables developers to build a fast, reliable, and clear test base. By structuring precise unit tests, simulating external behavior, and validating critical functions in real time, developers reduce risk, speed up development, and increase confidence in continuous delivery. A culture of automated testing, applied with discipline and technique, is both a competitive advantage and a non-negotiable requirement for any project that seeks professional quality.

CHAPTER 19. KOTLIN MULTIPLATFORM (KMP)

Kotlin Multiplatform is a modern and strategic approach that allows sharing business logic across different platforms such as Android, iOS, web, and backend, while still preserving platform-specific layers. This paradigm significantly reduces code duplication, centralizes business rules, and simplifies the maintenance of integrated, scalable, and complete solutions.

Unlike frameworks that aim to fully abstract native behavior, Kotlin Multiplatform is designed to reuse only the logic that can genuinely be common across platforms, while maintaining direct access to native resources and APIs through dedicated modules. This ensures a balance between cross-platform productivity and native performance.

Project Structure

A KMP project typically consists of:

- **commonMain module**: where shared business logic lives

- **Platform-specific modules** (e.g., androidMain, iosMain, jvmMain, jsMain): implement native dependencies

- **expect/actual blocks**: used to declare and implement platform-specific behavior

Initial Setup

Use the kotlin-multiplatform **plugin in your** build.gradle.kts:

kotlin

```
plugins {
    kotlin("multiplatform") version "1.9.0"
}

kotlin {
    android()
    iosX64()
    iosArm64()
    jvm()

    sourceSets {
        val commonMain by getting {
            dependencies {
                implementation("org.jetbrains.kotlinx:kotlinx-coroutines-core:1.7.3")
            }
        }
        val androidMain by getting
        val iosMain by creating {
            dependsOn(commonMain)
        }
    }
```

```
}
```

The sourceSets block organizes the code hierarchically. commonMain contains shared logic, while platform modules extend it with specific implementations.

expect/actual: Platform-Specific Implementations

- In commonMain:

kotlin

```
expect fun getUniqueIdentifier(): String
```

- In androidMain:

kotlin

```
actual fun getUniqueIdentifier(): String {
    return Settings.Secure.getString(context.contentResolver,
Settings.Secure.ANDROID_ID)
}
```

- In iosMain:

kotlin

```
actual fun getUniqueIdentifier(): String {
    return
UIDevice.currentDevice.identifierForVendor?.UUIDString ?:
"unknown"
```

```
}
```

This model maintains a unified interface while allowing native-optimized implementations. The compiler enforces that every expect declaration has a corresponding actual.

Shared Libraries

Libraries like kotlinx.coroutines, kotlinx.serialization, Ktor, and SQLDelight are KMP-compatible and can be used directly in commonMain.

Example with kotlinx.serialization:

kotlin

```kotlin
@Serializable
data class User(val id: Int, val name: String)


val json = Json.encodeToString(User(1, "Carlos"))
```

With Ktor for HTTP calls:

kotlin

```kotlin
val client = HttpClient {
    install(ContentNegotiation) {
        json()
    }
}


suspend fun loadData(): User {
    return client.get("https://api.myservice.com/user").body()
```

```
}
```

This code can reside in commonMain and is executed using native clients (OkHttp for Android, NSURLSession for iOS).

Sharing ViewModels and Domain Logic

KMP supports reusing ViewModels and domain logic. Libraries like KMP-NativeCoroutines, StateFlow, and cross-platform MVI architectures help structure reactive and cohesive applications.

Compilation and Artifacts

- **Android**: the shared code integrates as a module.

- **iOS**: output is a .framework consumable via Xcode, with integration through CocoaPods or Swift Package Manager.

kotlin

```kotlin
kotlin {
    ios {
        binaries {
            framework {
                baseName = "shared"
            }
        }
    }
}
```

In the iOS project's Podfile:

ruby

```
pod 'shared', :path => '../shared'
```

The generated code can be called from Swift or Objective-C with full interoperability.

Common Error Resolution

- Missing actual implementation for expect declarations
  Solution: Implement actual in androidMain, iosMain, and other targets

- Using libraries not compatible with Multiplatform
  Solution: Verify KMP compatibility before adding dependencies, favoring libraries that support commonMain

- Coupling UI logic with business logic in shared code
  Solution: Keep business rules and models in commonMain, leave UI in native layers

- Accessing native APIs directly in commonMain
  Solution: Use expect/actual blocks to encapsulate native calls

- Incorrect target configuration in build.gradle.kts
  Solution: Validate targets for all architectures (iosX64, iosArm64, jvm, etc.)

Best Practices

- Clearly organize the project into common, platform, and presentation layers

- Isolate business logic in commonMain using pure functions and immutable models

- Centralize networking, business rules, and data models in shared modules

- Use jvmTest to test shared logic before platform-specific integration

- Avoid over-abstraction that complicates native platform maintenance

- Reuse ViewModels and UseCases across platforms via common interfaces

- Keep dependencies up to date to follow KMP ecosystem evolution

- Prefer asynchronous communication using Flow or StateFlow

- Automate native artifact builds for team distribution

- Apply platform-specific integration tests to validate interaction with shared code

Strategic Summary

Kotlin Multiplatform represents a strategic leap in modern development, offering an elegant architecture for sharing logic across Android, iOS, and backend with safety, performance, and control. Smart use of expect/actual, multiplatform libraries, unified serialization, and coroutine-based async models enables robust, consistent applications across multiple environments with a single technical core. Mastering KMP elevates Kotlin developers into full multiplatform architects, ready to deliver integrated and sustainable solutions at scale.

CHAPTER 20. BUILDING ANDROID APPLICATIONS WITH KOTLIN

Developing Android applications with Kotlin is now the recommended and officially supported approach by the Android ecosystem. The language provides modern, safe, and highly productive syntax with direct integration into platform APIs. Building a functional app involves understanding the lifecycle of activities, managing the UI via XML layouts, interacting fluently with the interface using ViewBinding, displaying lists using RecyclerView, and crafting visual experiences with animations.

Activity and Fragment Lifecycle

The lifecycle of Activity and Fragment defines the states a screen goes through from creation to destruction. Understanding these states ensures correct UI handling, timely data loading, and resource cleanup to avoid memory leaks.

Main Activity lifecycle methods:

- onCreate() – initialize screen, set layout and initial data

- onStart() – screen is about to become visible

- onResume() – screen is in the foreground and interactive

- onPause() – another component takes UI focus

- onStop() – screen is no longer visible

- onDestroy() – screen is being permanently destroyed

Basic Activity implementation:

kotlin

```kotlin
class MainActivity : AppCompatActivity() {
    override fun onCreate(savedInstanceState: Bundle?) {
        super.onCreate(savedInstanceState)
        setContentView(R.layout.activity_main)
    }
}
```

ViewBinding

To safely interact with the UI without using findViewById, enable ViewBinding in build.gradle.kts:

kotlin

```kotlin
android {
    buildFeatures {
        viewBinding = true
    }
}
```

Use it in an Activity:

kotlin

```kotlin
class MainActivity : AppCompatActivity() {
    private lateinit var binding: ActivityMainBinding
```

```
override fun onCreate(savedInstanceState: Bundle?) {
    super.onCreate(savedInstanceState)
    binding = ActivityMainBinding.inflate(layoutInflater)
    setContentView(binding.root)

    binding.botaoEnviar.setOnClickListener {
        val nome = binding.campoNome.text.toString()
        binding.textoResultado.text = "Olá, $nome"
    }
}
}
```

This eliminates manual casting and runtime nullability/type errors.

RecyclerView for Lists

Use RecyclerView for high-performance list displays.

XML layout:

xml

```
<androidx.recyclerview.widget.RecyclerView
    android:id="@+id/listaUsuarios"
    android:layout_width="match_parent"
    android:layout_height="match_parent"/>
```

Model class:

kotlin

```kotlin
data class Usuario(val nome: String, val email: String)
```

Custom Adapter:

kotlin

```kotlin
class UsuarioAdapter(private val usuarios: List<Usuario>) :
    RecyclerView.Adapter<UsuarioAdapter.ViewHolder>() {


    inner class ViewHolder(itemView: View) :
    RecyclerView.ViewHolder(itemView) {
        val nome =
    itemView.findViewById<TextView>(R.id.textoNome)
        val email =
    itemView.findViewById<TextView>(R.id.textoEmail)
    }


    override fun onCreateViewHolder(parent: ViewGroup,
    viewType: Int): ViewHolder {
        val item = LayoutInflater.from(parent.context)
            .inflate(R.layout.item_usuario, parent, false)
        return ViewHolder(item)
    }


    override fun onBindViewHolder(holder: ViewHolder,
    position: Int) {
        val usuario = usuarios[position]
```

```kotlin
        holder.nome.text = usuario.nome
        holder.email.text = usuario.email
    }


    override fun getItemCount() = usuarios.size
}
```

Initialize in Activity:

kotlin

```kotlin
val lista = listOf(
    Usuario("Carlos", "carlos@email.com"),
    Usuario("Ana", "ana@email.com")
)


val adapter = UsuarioAdapter(lista)
binding.listaUsuarios.layoutManager =
LinearLayoutManager(this)
binding.listaUsuarios.adapter = adapter
```

Navigation Between Screens

Use Intent to switch screens:

kotlin

```kotlin
val intent = Intent(this, DetalheActivity::class.java)
intent.putExtra("nome", usuario.nome)
startActivity(intent)
```

Retrieve data in the target Activity:

kotlin

val nome = intent.getStringExtra("nome")

binding.textoDetalhe.text = nome

Animations and Transitions

Create visual feedback with ViewPropertyAnimator:

kotlin

```
binding.botaoEnviar.animate()
    .alpha(0f)
    .setDuration(500)
    .withEndAction {
        binding.botaoEnviar.visibility = View.GONE
    }
```

For screen transitions:

kotlin

```
startActivity(intent)
overridePendingTransition(R.anim.entrada, R.anim.saida)
```

For advanced effects, use **MotionLayout** within **ConstraintLayout** to coordinate declarative animations and gestures.

State Management and UI Architecture

Manage state across screens and configuration changes using:

- ViewModel

- SavedStateHandle

- Local persistence where necessary

Use LiveData or StateFlow for reactive updates to the UI.

Common Error Resolution

- Accessing views with findViewById without type/null checks
  Solution: Use ViewBinding for type-safe access

- Updating UI from a background thread
  Solution: Always execute UI operations on the Main Thread

- Forgetting to implement getItemCount() in RecyclerView
  Solution: Ensure the list size is updated properly

- Not notifying adapter after list changes
  Solution: Use notifyDataSetChanged() or DiffUtil

- Navigating between screens without checking for intent extras
  Solution: Validate with intent.hasExtra()

Best Practices

- Use ViewBinding for safer and more readable UI

interactions

- Separate UI logic and business logic with ViewModel and layered architecture

- Use RecyclerView with optimized ViewHolder and lean item layouts

- Avoid NestedScrollView with long lists — prefer RecyclerView

- Manage lifecycle cleanly with onResume, onPause, and onStop

- Use LiveData or StateFlow for reactive UI updates

- Keep animations short and purposeful

- Create reusable themes and styles for visual consistency

- Design adaptive layouts with ConstraintLayout and responsive dimensions

- Use Navigation Component for structured, type-safe navigation

Strategic Summary

Building Android apps with Kotlin is a powerful and efficient experience, based on a language that promotes clarity, safety, and productivity. Mastering the app lifecycle, creating responsive interfaces with ViewBinding, displaying optimized lists with RecyclerView, and enhancing interaction with strategic animations allows developers to build modern and scalable apps. Deep understanding of Android structures and tools, combined with Kotlin's fluency, leads to robust, intuitive, and professionally crafted mobile applications.

CHAPTER 21. BACKEND DEVELOPMENT WITH KTOR

Ktor is an asynchronous framework for backend application development in Kotlin. Created and maintained by JetBrains, Ktor enables the creation of efficient, scalable, and modern HTTP APIs with a coroutine-based architecture that favors performance without compromising readability. It is ideal for building microservices, mobile app backends, and REST API servers with authentication, route control, and direct integration with databases.

To start a Ktor project, the appropriate plugin is added to build.gradle.kts:

kotlin

```
plugins {
    kotlin("jvm") version "1.9.0"
    application
}


application {
    mainClass.set("com.exemplo.ApplicationKt")
}
```

The minimum dependencies for a functional server include:

kotlin

```kotlin
implementation("io.ktor:ktor-server-core:2.3.3")

implementation("io.ktor:ktor-server-netty:2.3.3")

implementation("io.ktor:ktor-server-content-
negotiation:2.3.3")

implementation("io.ktor:ktor-serialization-kotlinx-json:2.3.3")

implementation("ch.qos.logback:logback-classic:1.4.11")
```

The main function starts the server:

kotlin

```kotlin
fun main(args: Array<String>): Unit =
io.ktor.server.netty.EngineMain.main(args)
```

Server configuration is done in the application.conf **file:**

hocon

```hocon
ktor {
    deployment {
        port = 8080
    }
    application {
        modules = [com.exemplo.module]
    }
}
```

The basic structure of an API with Ktor uses routing **to declare endpoints:**

kotlin

```kotlin
fun Application.module() {
    install(ContentNegotiation) {
        json()
    }

    routing {
        get("/") {
            call.respondText("API Ktor Online")
        }

        post("/dados") {
            val entrada = call.receive<DadoEntrada>()
            call.respond(DadoSaida(mensagem = "Received: ${entrada.valor}"))
        }
    }
}
```

Data models are defined with kotlinx.serialization:

kotlin

```kotlin
@Serializable
data class DadoEntrada(val valor: String)


@Serializable
```

```kotlin
data class DadoSaida(val mensagem: String)
```

Middlewares in Ktor are known as plugins, and are added via the install method. Plugins like CallLogging, CORS, DefaultHeaders, Compression, and StatusPages allow for control over headers, responses, compression, logging, and global error handling.

kotlin

```kotlin
install(CallLogging)
install(DefaultHeaders)
install(CORS) {
    allowMethod(HttpMethod.Options)
    anyHost()
}
install(StatusPages) {
    exception<Throwable> { call, cause ->
        call.respond(HttpStatusCode.InternalServerError,
cause.localizedMessage)
    }
}
```

JWT authentication is integrated through the Authentication plugin. You need to add the dependency:

kotlin

```kotlin
implementation("io.ktor:ktor-server-auth:2.3.3")
implementation("io.ktor:ktor-server-auth-jwt:2.3.3")
```

Authentication configuration:

kotlin

```kotlin
install(Authentication) {
    jwt("auth-jwt") {
        realm = "ktor sample"
        verifier(
            JWT.require(Algorithm.HMAC256("secret-key"))
                .withIssuer("my-server")
                .build()
        )
        validate { credential ->
            if (credential.payload.getClaim("usuario").asString() !=
"") JWTPrincipal(credential.payload) else null
        }
    }
}
```

Protected route with authentication:

kotlin

```kotlin
authenticate("auth-jwt") {
    get("/protected") {
        val principal = call.principal<JWTPrincipal>()
        val usuario =
principal?.payload?.getClaim("usuario")?.asString()
        call.respondText("Access granted to $usuario")
```

```
    }
}
```

To issue JWT tokens, the java-jwt library is used:

kotlin

```
val token = JWT.create()
    .withIssuer("my-server")
    .withClaim("usuario", "admin")
    .sign(Algorithm.HMAC256("secret-key"))
```

Database integration is done with libraries like **Exposed**, a Kotlin DSL for SQL, or external JDBC/ORM libraries. With Exposed, add:

kotlin

```
implementation("org.jetbrains.exposed:exposed-core:0.43.0")
implementation("org.jetbrains.exposed:exposed-dao:0.43.0")
implementation("org.jetbrains.exposed:exposed-jdbc:0.43.0")
implementation("org.postgresql:postgresql:42.6.0")
```

Database connection:

kotlin

```
Database.connect(
    url = "jdbc:postgresql://localhost:5432/mydatabase",
    driver = "org.postgresql.Driver",
    user = "user",
```

```
    password = "password"
)
```

Table definition:

kotlin

```kotlin
object Usuarios : Table() {
    val id = integer("id").autoIncrement()
    val nome = varchar("nome", 255)
    override val primaryKey = PrimaryKey(id)
}
```

Data insertion:

kotlin

```kotlin
transaction {
    Usuarios.insert {
        it[nome] = "Carlos"
    }
}
```

Data query:

kotlin

```kotlin
val result = transaction {
    Usuarios.selectAll().map { it[Usuarios.nome] }
}
```

Using transaction {} ensures safe execution and automatic rollback in case of errors.

Common Error Resolution

- Failing to install ContentNegotiation and encountering errors when serializing JSON
  Solution: Install the plugin and configure kotlinx.serialization

- Ignoring credential validation in JWT and allowing invalid tokens
  Solution: Manually verify claims and check for expired tokens

- Making blocking calls without withContext(Dispatchers.IO)
  Solution: Wrap database or disk operations with withContext

- Not catching exceptions and exposing internal errors to the client
  Solution: Use StatusPages with controlled error messages

- Misconfiguring CORS, preventing external requests
  Solution: Enable anyHost() or configure allowed origins

Best Practices

- Isolate routes into specific files or classes using Route and install

- Create a repository layer to abstract database access

- Use separate DTOs and models for data input and output

- Explicitly validate input before persisting to the database

- Standardize error responses with clear structure and appropriate status codes

- Generate JWT tokens with expiration time and secure keys

- Apply authentication with the minimal scope per route (authenticate {})

- Use call.respond() clearly with typed models

- Organize middleware (plugins) into isolated configuration blocks

- Test routes with tools like Postman, Insomnia, or Ktor Client

Strategic Summary

Backend development with Ktor in Kotlin combines performance, readability, and native integration with the modern ecosystem. Its coroutine-based architecture, declarative routes, reusable middleware, and full support for authentication and persistence make Ktor a highly productive platform for building robust, reactive, and secure APIs. Mastering its tools transforms the Kotlin developer into a complete backend engineer, ready to architect RESTful solutions that are efficient, scalable, and professionally delivered.

CHAPTER 22. DEPENDENCY MANAGEMENT WITH GRADLE

Dependency management is a central step in any modern Kotlin project. Gradle is the standard tool adopted in the ecosystem, and its integration with Kotlin DSL offers a declarative, safe, and highly expressive syntax. By mastering project configuration with Kotlin DSL, organizing multiple modules, versioning libraries in a controlled way, and applying optimization strategies, the developer gains full control over the build and delivery pipeline.

The structure of a modern project using Gradle with Kotlin DSL starts with the settings.gradle.kts file, which defines the included modules:

kotlin

```
rootProject.name = "my-project"


include(":app")

include(":core")

include(":api")
```

Each module will have its own build.gradle.kts, allowing isolation and specialization of dependencies, configurations, and tasks. This multi-module model is recommended for projects that grow in scope and complexity, such as Android applications, multiplatform libraries, and backend systems with multiple services.

In the main module, using Kotlin DSL to configure the base project starts with:

kotlin

```
plugins {
    kotlin("jvm") version "1.9.0"
    application
}


repositories {
    mavenCentral()
}


dependencies {
    implementation(kotlin("stdlib"))
    testImplementation("org.junit.jupiter:junit-jupiter:5.10.0")
}
```

The kotlin("jvm") function sets up the plugin for Kotlin use in JVM-based applications. The mavenCentral() repository is where Gradle retrieves most dependencies, but additional repositories like google() or internal repositories can be included.

The organization of dependencies into groups (implementation, api, compileOnly, testImplementation) controls the visibility and scope of each library:

- implementation: adds the dependency only for the current module

- **api**: exposes the dependency to other modules that consume this one

- **compileOnly**: compiles with the dependency, but does not include it at runtime

- **testImplementation**: used only in test code

Version definitions can be centralized in a libs.versions.toml file using the **version catalogs** feature:

toml

```toml
[versions]
kotlin = "1.9.0"
junit = "5.10.0"


[libraries]
kotlin-stdlib = { module = "org.jetbrains.kotlin:kotlin-stdlib", version.ref = "kotlin" }
junit = { module = "org.junit.jupiter:junit-jupiter", version.ref = "junit" }
```

In the build.gradle.kts, the dependency is referenced as:

kotlin

```kotlin
dependencies {
    implementation(libs.kotlin.stdlib)
    testImplementation(libs.junit)
}
```

This model encourages consistency and simplifies updates. All version modifications occur in a single location, avoiding duplication and inconsistency between modules.

In multiplatform projects with KMP, each sourceSet block has its own set of dependencies, and the build structure with Kotlin DSL facilitates this control:

kotlin

```kotlin
kotlin {
    jvm()
    ios()


    sourceSets {
        val commonMain by getting {
            dependencies {
                implementation("org.jetbrains.kotlinx:kotlinx-coroutines-core:1.7.3")
            }
        }
        val jvmMain by getting
        val iosMain by getting
    }
}
```

Build process optimization is an important technical differentiator. Gradle allows applying various strategies to reduce compilation time, avoid unnecessary recompilations, and improve overall build performance.

Enable parallel build:

properties

```
org.gradle.parallel=true
```

Enable local build cache:

properties

```
org.gradle.caching=true
```

Use precompiled configuration with build-logic and internal plugins:

kotlin

```
plugins {
    id("myproject.android-config")
}
```

Separate tasks between modules for independent execution using **configuration on demand**.

Using custom plugins also allows reusing configurations across different projects or teams. An internal plugin can be declared as:

kotlin

```
class AndroidConfigPlugin : Plugin<Project> {
    override fun apply(target: Project) {
        with(target) {
            plugins.apply("com.android.application")
```

```
        plugins.apply("kotlin-android")
    }
  }
}
```

Publishing internal libraries with controlled versioning is done with the maven-publish plugin. When configuring the publication:

kotlin

```
publishing {
    publications {
        create<MavenPublication>("release") {
            groupId = "com.company"
            artifactId = "my-library"
            version = "1.0.0"
            from(components["java"])
        }
    }
}
```

This allows modules to be published to an internal repository such as Artifactory, Nexus, or GitHub Packages, and consumed by other projects:

kotlin

```
repositories {
    maven {
```

```
    url = uri("https://repo.company.com/maven")
  }
}
```

Using custom tasks with Kotlin DSL also extends the power of Gradle. A task to clean cache or prepare data can be defined as:

kotlin

```
tasks.register("prepareData") {
  group = "automation"
  description = "Generates input data for the application"
  doLast {
    println("Data generated successfully.")
  }
}
```

For Android projects, the Gradle Kotlin DSL replaces the old build.gradle with clarity and strong typing. Example configuration in build.gradle.kts:

kotlin

```
android {
  compileSdk = 34

  defaultConfig {
    applicationId = "com.example.app"
    minSdk = 21
    targetSdk = 34
```

```
    versionCode = 1

    versionName = "1.0"

}


buildTypes {

    release {

        isMinifyEnabled = true

        proguardFiles(

            getDefaultProguardFile("proguard-android-
optimize.txt"),

            "proguard-rules.pro"

        )

    }

  }

}
```

This structure makes the project more maintainable, validated at edit time, and with intelligent autocomplete.

Common Error Resolution

- Defining library versions directly in multiple files
  Solution: Centralize versions using Version Catalogs or project properties

- Using compile instead of implementation
  Solution: Migrate to modern scopes for proper dependency

isolation

- Failing to declare repositories when adding a new dependency
  Solution: Ensure mavenCentral() or the correct repository is listed

- Placing complex build logic directly in build.gradle.kts
  Solution: Extract to plugins or modular configuration files

- Mixing Groovy and Kotlin DSL in the same project
  Solution: Use Kotlin DSL exclusively for consistency and validation

Best Practices

- Organize projects into multiple modules with clear responsibilities

- Centralize dependency versions using libs.versions.toml files
- Use implementation instead of api, except in public libraries

- Reuse build logic with internal custom plugins

- Use buildSrc to abstract repeated tasks and configurations

- Enable caching and parallel build for better performance

- Write custom tasks with doFirst and doLast for precise control

- Automate library publishing with maven-publish

- Adopt semantic versioning (SemVer) in internal libraries

- Test build changes in CI with pipelines separated by module

Strategic Summary

Dependency management with Gradle and Kotlin DSL represents a revolution in productivity and scalability for Kotlin projects. By structuring projects in multiple modules, centralizing versions, optimizing builds, and configuring tasks with declarative clarity, the developer builds robust and flexible delivery pipelines. Mastering this layer ensures control over build quality, accelerates the development cycle, and establishes an environment ready for continuous growth with a high professional standard.

CHAPTER 23. BEST PRACTICES AND CODING STANDARDS

The adoption of best practices and code patterns is a non-negotiable technical requirement for any project aiming for maintainability, readability, and scalability. Kotlin was designed with a clear and expressive syntax that favors writing clean code, but this does not dispense with engineering discipline. Careful naming, continuous refactoring, consistent formatting, proper application of design patterns, and the definition of a solid architecture form the foundation for sustainable projects.

Code clarity begins with naming choices. Names of variables, functions, classes, and packages should be descriptive, concise, and contextual. Variables should clearly indicate what they represent:

kotlin

```kotlin
val isActiveUser: Boolean
val totalItems: Int
val filePath: String
```

Functions should follow the naming convention with verbs, making clear what they do:

kotlin

```kotlin
fun calculateAverage(): Double
fun findUserById(id: Int): User?
```

Classes and objects should use noun names representing domain concepts:

kotlin

```
class Order

class AuthenticationController
```

Consistency in naming between files, classes, and methods reduces the reading curve and avoids ambiguity between system elements.

Refactoring is a continuous practice that improves the internal structure of the code without changing its external behavior. Small, frequent refactorings are preferable to drastic rewrites and should be guided by automated tests that ensure the integrity of the application.

Recommended refactorings include:

- Extracting long functions into smaller, well-named methods

- Removing duplicated code with reusable helper functions

- Replacing nested control structures with when or early return

- Applying sealed class for structures that require exhaustive control

- Using extension functions to encapsulate recurring behaviors

Code formatting should follow a unified standard. Tools

like ktlint or detekt ensure that all formatting, indentation, and spacing rules are automatically applied. This reduces subjective debates in code reviews and strengthens codebase standardization.

Key formatting recommendations:

- Use 4-space indentation

- Limit lines to a maximum of 100 characters

- Break long expressions into multiple aligned lines

- Avoid excessive nested blocks

- Use spaces after commas and binary operators

- Keep blank lines between logical code blocks

- Avoid redundant comments; prefer self-explanatory code

Correct use of val and var is a sign of technical maturity. Whenever possible, use val to reinforce immutability and make data flow reasoning easier:

kotlin

```kotlin
val result = processInput(input)
```

Beyond general practices, proper use of design patterns helps organize the system in a cohesive and predictable way. Patterns should be applied with clear purpose and not as automatic conventions.

Recommended patterns for Kotlin:

Singleton: Applied with object to represent global and unique instances:

```kotlin
object Settings {
    val version = "1.0"
}
```

Factory: Used to encapsulate object creation with conditional logic:

```kotlin
interface Document
class Report : Document
class Contract : Document

object DocumentFactory {
    fun create(type: String): Document = when (type) {
        "report" -> Report()
        "contract" -> Contract()
        else -> throw IllegalArgumentException("Unknown type")
    }
}
```

Strategy: Ideal for replacing conditionals with interchangeable behaviors:

```kotlin
interface Operation {
    fun execute(a: Int, b: Int): Int
```

```
}


class Addition : Operation {
    override fun execute(a: Int, b: Int) = a + b
}


class Subtraction : Operation {
    override fun execute(a: Int, b: Int) = a - b
}
```

Observer: Used to notify multiple objects of state changes:

kotlin

```
interface Observer {
    fun update()
}


class Subject {
    private val observers = mutableListOf<Observer>()


    fun add(o: Observer) {
        observers.add(o)
    }


    fun notifyAll() {
```

```
    observers.forEach { it.update() }
  }
}
```

Mastering architecture is the next step after mastering syntax. Kotlin is compatible with multiple architectural approaches, from traditional layered models to modern patterns like Clean Architecture and Hexagonal Architecture.

Recommended structure for layered applications:

- **Domain layer:** business rules and entities

- **Data layer:** database access, remote services, repositories

- **Presentation layer:** user interface, ViewModels, controllers

Separation of concerns between layers avoids cyclic dependencies, facilitates testing, and improves application scalability.

Specific best practices in project structure:

- Organize packages by function (domain, data, ui), not by type (classes, enums, utils)

- Isolate business logic in pure, testable functions

- Use interfaces to decouple dependencies

- Avoid direct access to infrastructure (database, network) in upper layers

- Keep functions small, cohesive, and with a single

responsibility

- Use sealed class to model states and controlled responses

- Favor composition over inheritance whenever possible

Common Error Resolution

- Naming variables generically or ambiguously like data, info, response
  Solution: Use names that clearly indicate the value's purpose

- Writing long functions with multiple responsibilities
  Solution: Refactor into smaller, more expressive functions

- Accessing global objects directly in multiple parts of the code
  Solution: Encapsulate access and inject dependencies

- Ignoring lint warnings and inconsistent formatting
  Solution: Adopt automatic tools like ktlint, detekt, and spotless

- Applying unnecessary design patterns in simple contexts
  Solution: Evaluate whether the pattern solves a real design problem

Best Practices

- Write readable code before seeking premature performance

- Name everything with clear intent: functions, variables, classes, and packages

- Refactor continuously, even in small delivery cycles

- Write functions with up to 15 lines that perform a single task

- Use val by default; use var only when there's a clear reason

- Apply extension functions to make utilities more readable

- Use sealed class to model state or controlled responses

- Apply automated testing from the domain layer

- Keep responsibilities separated by technical or business context

- Reuse structures and patterns validated by the Kotlin community

Strategic Summary

Best practices and code patterns in Kotlin raise the technical quality level of the project. Clarity in naming, layered code organization, application of appropriate patterns, and disciplined refactoring build solid, readable, and easily maintainable systems. By adopting a strategic approach centered on readability and predictability, the developer gains productivity, reduces evolution costs, and strengthens the architectural foundation of the application with consistency and security. Code becomes not just a delivery tool, but a strategic asset of engineering.

CHAPTER 24. PUBLISHING KOTLIN PROJECTS

Publishing a Kotlin project professionally requires technical mastery of packaging, documentation, versioning, and distribution. Publishing to repositories such as Maven Central ensures visibility, reuse, and integration with other applications. In addition, the automatic generation of documentation with Dokka and the application of technical promotion strategies expand reach and strengthen the credibility of the project. A good publication cycle turns a private repository into a reusable, tested, and respected component within the community.

The process begins with the proper configuration of the project in Gradle using Kotlin DSL. A published project must provide clear information about the group, name, version, and artifacts. The minimum configuration in build.gradle.kts includes:

kotlin

```
group = "com.yourproject"
version = "1.0.0"

plugins {
    kotlin("jvm") version "1.9.0"
    `maven-publish`
    signing
```

```
}
```

The maven-publish plugin is responsible for creating the .pom, .jar, and .module files used by Maven Central and other repositories. The basic publication structure can be configured as follows:

kotlin

```kotlin
publishing {
    publications {
        create<MavenPublication>("release") {
            from(components["java"])

            groupId = "com.yourproject"
            artifactId = "library"
            version = "1.0.0"

            pom {
                name.set("Kotlin Library")
                description.set("A library to do X with Kotlin")
                url.set("https://github.com/yourproject/library")

                licenses {
                    license {
                        name.set("MIT License")
                        url.set("https://opensource.org/licenses/MIT")
                    }
```

```
            }

        developers {
            developer {
                id.set("devname")
                name.set("Your Name")
                email.set("your@email.com")
            }
        }


        scm {
            connection.set("scm:git:git://github.com/
yourproject/library.git")
            developerConnection.set("scm:git:ssh://
github.com/yourproject/library.git")
            url.set("https://github.com/yourproject/library")
        }
      }
     }
   }
}
```

Publishing to Maven Central requires credentials, digital signing, and synchronization with Sonatype's central repository. The first step is to create an account on Sonatype Jira, request access to the namespace, and configure the data in gradle.properties:

properties

```
signing.keyId=KEYID
signing.password=KEY_PASSWORD
signing.secretKeyRingFile=/path/to/secret.asc


ossrhUsername=YOUR_USERNAME
ossrhPassword=YOUR_PASSWORD
```

These credentials are referenced in Gradle:

kotlin

```kotlin
signing {
    sign(publishing.publications["release"])
}


publishing {
    repositories {
        maven {
            name = "ossrh"
            url = uri("https://oss.sonatype.org/service/local/staging/deploy/maven2/")
            credentials {
                username = findProperty("ossrhUsername") as String

                password = findProperty("ossrhPassword") as String
            }
```

```
    }
  }
}
```

With everything configured, local publishing can be tested with:

bash

```
./gradlew publishToMavenLocal
```

And publishing to Maven Central is done with:

bash

```
./gradlew publish
```

All .jar and .pom artifacts must be digitally signed with GPG, and the package validation is done automatically by Sonatype before the final release. Once approved, the artifact is synchronized with Maven Central and becomes available to any project that references its groupId and artifactId.

Technical documentation of the project is generated with Dokka, JetBrains' official generator for Kotlin projects. It converts KDoc comments into HTML, Markdown, or Javadoc-compatible formats. Inclusion in build.gradle.kts is done with:

kotlin

```
plugins {
    id("org.jetbrains.dokka") version "1.8.20"
}
```

The task to generate HTML documentation:

bash

```
./gradlew dokkaHtml
```

Or for Markdown:

bash

```
./gradlew dokkaGfm
```

The output can be hosted on any static page service, such as GitHub Pages, GitLab Pages, or Vercel. It is highly recommended that the documentation be updated with each published version, including usage examples, requirements, and integration instructions.

In addition to technical documentation, promotion strategies are essential to increase library usage. Effective actions include:

- Publishing source code with a detailed README on GitHub

- Creating full integration examples with real projects

- Creating status badges like build, test coverage, and latest version

- Publishing tutorials on Dev.to, Medium, Hashnode, or community repositories

- Sharing the library in forums such as Reddit, Hacker News, and Kotlin groups

- Announcing updates on technical social media such as LinkedIn and Twitter

- Registering the library in public catalogs like Kotlin

Weekly, Android Arsenal, or Awesome Kotlin

Applying semantic versioning (semver) is mandatory so that users understand the impact of updates:

- MAJOR version change for breaking changes

- MINOR version for new compatible features

- PATCH version for internal fixes and adjustments

Changelog generation can be automated with tools like git-chglog, release-it, or direct integration with GitHub Releases.

Common Error Resolution

- Forgetting to sign artifacts before publishing
  Solution: Use the signing plugin and provide a valid GPG key

- Failing to correctly fill in the pom block in
  MavenPublication
  Solution: Add all mandatory information for project, license, and SCM

- Using an artifact name already registered by another organization
  Solution: Request a unique namespace on Sonatype Jira before publishing

- Omitting README, LICENSE, and instructions in the public repository
  Solution: Keep these files in the root of the project with up-to-date content

- Publishing unstable versions as 1.0.0 without tests or documentation
  Solution: Use 0.x.y until the project reaches real maturity

Best Practices

- Use semantic versioning consistently and with discipline

- Sign all artifacts and validate them locally before publishing

- Automate publishing with CI/CD scripts and pipelines

- Generate documentation with Dokka and publish it along with the version

- Maintain a complete README with usage examples and installation instructions

- Provide changelogs for each release with clear change logs

- Reuse dependencies with api or implementation transparently

- Respond to issues and questions quickly to build community trust

- Ensure test coverage before every release

- Validate artifacts with publishToMavenLocal and integration tests

Strategic Summary

Publishing Kotlin projects with professional quality requires more than pushing code to a repository. It involves technical planning, version control, secure packaging, and accessible documentation. Publishing to Maven Central, combined with automatic documentation generation with Dokka and targeted promotion strategies, turns the library into a reusable and respected component. By mastering this flow, the developer not only delivers reusable code but also positions their solution as a relevant part of the Kotlin ecosystem.

CHAPTER 25. EXPLORING THE FUTURE WITH KOTLIN

Kotlin is not just an established language for Android development or backend applications on the JVM. It strategically positions itself in the current and future landscape of software engineering, offering native support for multiple platforms, integration with emerging technologies, and a technical structure that fosters continuous innovation. Its advancement within the modern ecosystem shows that Kotlin is at the center of a profound transformation: unified, performant, reactive, and multiplatform development—without sacrificing clarity or productivity.

The main technical trend associated with the language is its consolidation as a foundational technology for multiplatform applications. With Kotlin Multiplatform (KMP), it becomes possible to share business logic, authentication logic, validation, persistence, and REST services between Android, iOS, web, and backend. At the same time, full access to each system's native resources is preserved. This approach has attracted companies seeking operational efficiency without compromising user experience on their platforms.

Support for expect and actual, combined with the maturity of tools like Ktor, Kotlinx.serialization, SQLDelight, and Coroutines, makes it viable to centralize system logic in a single Kotlin core. The clear trend is the growth of composed architectures with a shared base and minimalist native frontends, optimizing maintainability and development time.

Another evolution vector is the rise of Jetpack Compose, the declarative toolkit for building Android interfaces that is also being extended to desktop and web via Compose Multiplatform. UI construction based on reactive states and immutability replaces the traditional imperative model and represents a paradigm shift in how modern interfaces are developed.

In Compose, the interface is described as a pure function:

kotlin

```kotlin
@Composable
fun Greeting(name: String) {
    Text(text = "Hello, $name!")
}
```

This function is automatically re-evaluated whenever the name parameter changes. The trend is for Compose to become the standard way of writing native, reactive, and multiplatform interfaces with Kotlin, directly impacting application layer architecture and event flow.

In the execution environment, Kotlin extends its reach with WebAssembly (WASM), a compact binary format executed directly in the browser without plugins. Projects like kotlin-wasm already allow compiling Kotlin code directly to WASM, opening possibilities for the same codebase to be used both in backends and high-performance native frontends. The trend is the emergence of libraries and tools that will allow writing rich web experiences in Kotlin, maintaining the language's strong typing and functional model.

Kotlin is also positioning itself as an orchestration interface for artificial intelligence, machine learning, and cognitive automation solutions. Frameworks like KotlinDL already offer direct APIs for building neural networks, image processing, and supervised classification. Furthermore, Kotlin natively interacts with libraries written in Python or Java, making it an elegant control hub for complex data and decision flows.

In practice, a simple classifier using KotlinDL can be defined as:

kotlin

```
val model = Sequential.of(
    Input(28, 28, 1),
    Conv2D(16, kernelSize = 3),
    MaxPool2D(),
    Flatten(),
    Dense(128),
    Output(10)
)
```

This code reflects the clarity of the language, even in highly complex technical scenarios.

The growth of Web3 and distributed solutions also aligns with Kotlin's rise. The language can be used as a foundation for lightweight clients, mobile apps with integrated wallets, governance dashboards, integrations with smart contracts via REST API, and decentralized data indexers. The focus is on robust, responsive, secure, and interoperable clients— characteristics where Kotlin delivers excellent results.

In the blockchain context, integration with signature libraries, transaction decoding, hashing, and node communication is facilitated by Kotlin's interoperability with Java, as well as native support for cryptography and binary manipulation. This positions Kotlin as an ideal language for auxiliary Web3 infrastructure components.

Kotlin's presence is also growing in the Internet of Things (IoT) field, especially in embedded Android devices, industrial applications using Android Things, intelligent edge solutions, and applications connected to sensors. Combined with asynchronous libraries, native sockets, and device control via Android APIs, Kotlin enables the construction of automation, telemetry, and distributed analytics solutions quickly and reliably.

The future trend indicates that Kotlin will operate at all levels of system architecture:

- High-performance backend with Ktor

- Reactive frontend with Compose Web or multiplatform

- Embedded devices with Kotlin/Native

- AI orchestration layers with KotlinDL

- Decentralized applications with blockchain and mobile SDKs

- Unified data models with Kotlin Multiplatform

- Browser execution with Kotlin WebAssembly

- Command-line tools with Kotlin CLI

- Connected services using coroutines and asynchronous flow

Beyond technical expansion, the Kotlin ecosystem is growing in governance. The community is active, with open contributions, recurring technical events, and evolution driven by fast feedback cycles. The incremental innovation model allows projects to adopt new features without breaking compatibility.

The language also reinforces its position as a modern engineering education tool. Its smooth learning curve, combined with advanced features, supports both basic logic teaching and advanced topics like distributed computing, concurrency, and AI.

Common Error Resolution

- Assuming Kotlin is limited to Android
  Solution: Study and apply the multiplatform and server-side Kotlin ecosystem

- Ignoring Compose's potential and continuing with XML by inertia
  Solution: Gradually migrate flows to reactive declarative UI

- Disregarding the need for true multiplatform in modern solutions
  Solution: Apply KMP for business logic, validation, persistence, and networking

- Forcing architectures from other languages that don't respect Kotlin's idioms
  Solution: Design systems based on Kotlin's idiomatic features

- Failing to keep up with official language and tool updates
  Solution: Monitor KotlinLang releases, GitHub activity, and the JetBrains roadmap

Best Practices

- Adopt multiplatform as the foundational structure for new projects

- Use Compose for reactive, state-synchronized interfaces

- Explore KotlinDL, kotlinx.serialization, kotlinx.coroutines, and Ktor for modern solutions

- Invest in expect/actual to maintain platform flexibility

- Generate automated documentation and multiplatform tests from the start

- Use Kotlin as an orchestration layer in systems with multiple languages

- Integrate WebAssembly as a lightweight alternative to JavaScript in critical components

- Build scalable REST APIs and WebSockets with Ktor and coroutines

- Use Kotlin in mobile SDKs for blockchain-based services

- Leverage native support for functional and reactive programming to reduce coupling

Strategic Summary

Kotlin is establishing itself as a central language in both the present and future of software engineering. Its technical structure, multiplatform support, integration with emerging technologies, and syntactic consistency elevate the development standard and reduce platform barriers. Mastery of Kotlin today is a competitive advantage, but soon it will become a fundamental skill for those who wish to lead technological projects with real impact across all fronts—from cloud to device, backend to AI, mobile to blockchain. Kotlin is not just a language choice: it's a vision of the future.

FINAL CONCLUSION

Learning Kotlin goes far beyond mastering its syntax—it involves building a solid technical foundation capable of supporting modern, multiplatform, scalable, and performance-oriented solutions. Each chapter of this manual was designed to strengthen your practical skills, consolidate sound architectural decisions, and prepare you for the real-world challenges of the tech industry.

In Chapter 1, we explored Kotlin's origins, advantages, and use cases, establishing a clear understanding of its ecosystem and Java interoperability. Chapter 2 guided you through the complete setup of your development environment, emphasizing productivity and technical fluency with IntelliJ IDEA and Android Studio.

Chapter 3 introduced Kotlin's foundational structure, focusing on type inference, functions, and essential constructs. In Flow Control (Chapter 4), you learned to manage conditional logic and repetition with idiomatic constructs like if, when, for, and while.

In Chapter 5, function construction was expanded with lambdas, scope functions (let, apply, run), and default parameters. Chapter 6 focused on manipulating collections using functional operations, while Chapter 7 covered modeling with classes, objects, and properties.

Object-oriented mastery was deepened in Chapters 8 and 9, encompassing inheritance, polymorphism, interfaces, abstract classes, and reusable contracts. Chapter 10 introduced string manipulation using interpolation, regex, and multiline strings.

In Chapter 11, you structured file reading and writing with safety and performance in mind. Chapter 12 explored exception handling, including try, catch, finally, validation, and custom exception creation.

The object-oriented conceptual base was consolidated in Chapter 13 and extended into functional programming in Chapter 14, emphasizing pure functions, immutability, map, reduce, and composition.

With Chapter 15, the asynchronous journey began: launch, async, await, withContext, and Dispatchers laid the foundation for non-blocking applications. Chapter 16 connected your code to the real world via REST integration using Retrofit and Ktor, JSON handling, and JWT authentication.

In Chapter 17, local persistence was handled with SQLite and Room, covering the full CRUD cycle, advanced queries, and relationships. Unit testing, integration, mocking with MockK, and testing practices were addressed in Chapter 18, reinforcing solution reliability.

Chapter 19 introduced the power of Kotlin Multiplatform (KMP), including the commonMain structure, expect/actual, and Android, iOS, and backend integration. In Android Applications with Kotlin (Chapter 20), you mastered lifecycle management, ViewBinding, RecyclerView, and reactive animations.

Complete backend development was structured in Chapter 21 using Ktor, covering APIs, routes, middleware, authentication, and database integration. Chapter 22 focused on build engineering with Gradle Kotlin DSL, modularization, versioning, and optimization.

Best practices and coding standards were solidified in Chapter 23, emphasizing clean code, naming conventions, refactoring, formatting, and design pattern application. Chapter 24 presented the professional publication cycle, including Maven

Central, signing, Dokka, and targeted promotion strategies.

Finally, Chapter 25 projected Kotlin's future in the multiplatform landscape—declarative with Compose, interoperable with WebAssembly, and strategic for AI, Blockchain, and IoT—cementing Kotlin as the central language of the next technological cycle.

Mastering all these areas exponentially increases your ability to design, develop, test, publish, and scale robust solutions across multiple domains. Whether you're building mobile apps, backend APIs, distributed SDKs, or technical tools, mastering Kotlin opens up concrete paths for innovation, technical leadership, and market relevance.

We deeply thank you for trusting this material. Our mission is to transform technical knowledge into real, applicable, and lasting advantage.

Sincerely,
Diego Rodrigues & Team!